Y(.

Talking Heads

Alan Bennett

Notes by Delia Dick

 Longman   York Press

Extracts from *Talking Heads* by kind permission of The Peters Fraser and Dunlop
Group Ltd on behalf of Alan Bennett

YORK PRESS
322 Old Brompton Road, London SW5 9JH

PEARSON EDUCATION LIMITED
Edinburgh Gate, Harlow,
Essex CM20 2JE, United Kingdom
Associated companies, branches and representatives throughout the world

First published 1999

ISBN 0–582–41468–7

Designed by Vicki Pacey
Phototypeset by Gem Graphics, Trenance, Mawgan Porth, Cornwall
Colour reproduction and film output by Spectrum Colour
Produced by Addison Wesley Longman China Limited, Hong Kong

CONTENTS

PART ONE

INTRODUCTION

HOW TO STUDY A PLAY

Studying on your own requires self-discipline and a carefully thought-out work plan in order to be effective.

- Drama is a special kind of writing (the technical term is 'genre') because it needs a performance in the theatre to arrive at a full interpretation of its meaning. Try to imagine that you are a member of the audience when reading the play. Think about how it could be presented on the stage, not just about the words on the page.

- Drama is always about conflict of some sort (which may be below the surface). Identify the conflicts in the play and you will be close to identifying the large ideas or themes which bind all the parts together.

- Make careful notes on themes, character, plot and any sub-plots of the play.

- Why do you like or dislike the characters in the play? How do your feelings towards them develop and change?

- Playwrights find non-realistic ways of allowing an audience to see into the minds and motives of their characters, for example soliloquy, aside or music. Consider how such dramatic devices are used in the play you are studying.

- Think of the playwright writing the play. Why were these particular arrangements of events, characters and speeches chosen?

- Cite exact sources for all quotations, whether from the text itself or from critical commentaries. Wherever possible find your own examples from the play to back up your opinions.

- Always express your ideas in your own words.

This York Note offers an introduction to *Talking Heads* and cannot substitute for close reading of the text and the study of secondary sources.

The narrators of Alan Bennett's six monologues for television, *Talking Heads*, are ordinary people – ordinary to the point of dullness – and their self-absorbed gossip might be considered tedious under other circumstances. And yet Alan Bennett has made these accounts of what he called 'ordinary, uneventful, desperate' (*Radio Times*, 16–22 April, 1988) lives absolutely riveting.

We meet six characters, each with a tale to tell, and their stories are both terrible and very funny. Domesticated bachelor Graham fears that he is going to lose his mental balance and his mother when she seems about to leave him for an old flame. Susan, the vicar's wife, has a quarrel with Jesus which drives her to drink, and Irene's poison-pen activities land her in prison. Lesley, the bit-part actress, manages to ignore the fact that her 'big chance' actually involves a nude role in a pornographic movie rather than serious acting; it suits Muriel, a middle-class woman recently widowed, to be oblivious to the real natures of her husband and son. Doris makes a last stand in the home she sees as an outpost in the battle against dirt and disorder.

'Gossip as drama' is a phrase which has been used of Alan Bennett's television work and he has a keen ear for the nuances of trivial conversation. His dialogue retains total authenticity, whilst he reworks and heightens it for dramatic and usually tragicomic purposes. He captures the minutiae of everyday life over and over again, by references to details he has stored away – sometimes from his childhood days. For instance – Alan Bennett tells us in his 'Introduction' to *Talking Heads* – Wilfred's ambition, in *A Cream Cracker Under the Settee*, to take up fretwork and make toys and money, is based on a memory of Alan Bennett's father and the toys he made for his sons in the Second World War. In *Bed Among the Lentils*, Susan's narrative brings in quotations from the Book of Common Prayer; the author recalls in his autobiographical *Writing Home* (Faber, 1994) that this was a work from which he had 'learned large sections by heart' as a devout Anglican when he was young. Like Susan, he became an agnostic but nevertheless still finds the language compelling. Again in his 'Introduction' the author traces his account of Susan's shaken belief to a timid *grafitto* in a school hymn book, which said, 'Get lost, Jesus'.

Alan Bennett is very much a northerner, as his writing often demonstrates. Other sources of material, however, are related to what he calls his 'metropolitan' aspect. He mentions that the funeral of Muriel Carpenter's husband in *Soldiering On* was suggested by that of a friend's father who, too, had 'touched upon life at many points'. Lesley, he claims, also in the 'Introduction', is based upon many unsuccessful small-part actors he has seen auditioned, whose estimation of the importance of their previous work bears little relation to fact. In *Writing Home* he describes how in New York in 1980 he was persuaded to attend a 'theatrical experience', which turned out to be an Alcoholics Anonymous meeting: 'My name is Barbara, I am an alcoholic' and so on – obviously useful in *Bed Among the Lentils*.

The intimacy of the television screen has offered opportunities in *Talking Heads* which Alan Bennett has been able to realise fully. The economy of the form may have appealed, as has been suggested, to the BBC in the financial difficulties which began in the Eighties, but it also demonstrated the author's ability to pull off a *tour de force* within constrained limits. The plays, too, demand accomplished actors and those involved met the challenge. Students of these texts may well have to read them as short stories, if video or audio tapes are not readily accessible. The plays are sometimes performed on the stage and you may be lucky enough to see a performance of one or more. Desirable as it is to see plays in performance, however, the texts of *Talking Heads* do stand very well by themselves: as Alan Bennett says in his 'Introduction', there is 'a single point of view, with 'a sole narrator in each play'. As he comments, the experience of watching a narrative told by one actor is more like reading a short story than watching a play. Since so much of the story involves people and events not seen by the viewer, an effort of imagination similar to that required in reading a story has to come into play.

PART TWO

Summaries & Commentaries

The text is that of Alan Bennett, *Talking Heads*, BBC Books, 1988, and the video of the same name by BBC Television Productions, 1988. The video contains:

A Chip in the Sugar GRAHAM – Alan Bennett, directed by Stuart Burge

Bed Among the Lentils SUSAN – Maggie Smith, directed by Alan Bennett

A Lady of Letters IRENE RUDDOCK – Patricia Routledge, directed by Giles Foster

Her Big Chance LESLEY – Julie Walters, directed by Giles Foster

Soldiering On MURIEL – Stephanie Cole, directed by Tristram Powell

A Cream Cracker Under the Sofa DORIS – Thora Hird, directed by Stuart Burge

A Chip in the Sugar

Synopsis

Graham Whittaker lives with his seventy-two year old mother, Vera. Graham runs the house and looks after Mrs Whittaker, who is rather forgetful, but spirited and still lively enough to enjoy outings and occasional visits to small restaurants or cafés. She likes to thinks that she and Graham can be taken for husband and wife when they are out. Graham reads the *Guardian*, has modest tastes and is knowledgeable about the history of architecture; his mother seems to share his interests. One day when they are out Mrs Whittaker has a fall. She is helped by a long lost friend, who happens to be passing by. Frank Turnbull leads the way to a flashy café and flirts with Vera, whom it appears he knew well in the days before she was married to Graham's father. He is a men's outfitter with vulgar tastes and is rude to Graham about his old-fashioned style of dress. He is dismissive about Graham's difficulties after Vera explains to him that her son has mental health problems.

Graham finds it hard to come to terms with his mother's rekindled interest in her old admirer and discusses his feelings – unprofitably – with the members of a therapy group which he attends. Frank Turnbull's courtship continues and Graham's foremost place in his mother's affections is in danger; he is particularly dismayed by her disloyalty in rapidly adopting the views and interests of the reactionary Frank Turnbull. Soon Mrs Whittaker drops the bombshell that she and Turnbull are to be married: Graham will have to move out of their home and live in a hostel. Graham's wretchedness is made worse by his belief that some of the earlier symptoms of his illness are returning; he thinks that someone is knocking at the door and that the house is being watched, but fears that he may be suffering from delusions. However, he is not mistaken. When his mother is out with Frank Turnbull, buying last minute items to take on their honeymoon, he eventually opens the door after there has been some persistent knocking and shouting through the letter-box: the visitor is Turnbull's daughter, who brings news that delights Graham. He is vindicated in his intense dislike of his mother's admirer, as he is able to tell her that Frank has an invalid wife and has deceived other women as well as her. Mrs Whittaker is deeply upset and reveals that she has found life dull and with her son, whom she accuses of abnormality and of enjoying pornographic magazines.

Mrs Whittaker's attack on Graham is short-lived; within a day or two their previous domestic relationship is re-established.

SCENE 1 (PP. 16–20)   Mrs Whittaker meets an old admirer

The sparsely furnished bedroom of the narrator, Graham Whittaker.

Graham, 'a mild, middle-aged man' (p. 16), remembers how the previous day he and his elderly mother had been out in town when Mrs Whittaker had fallen on the pavement as Graham had been trying to disengage her unnecessarily clinging arm from his. One of the helpful passers-by was Frank Turnbull, a long-lost friend of Mrs Whittaker from before her marriage, and apparently an early admirer – 'pre-Dad' (p. 16) – of whose existence Graham had been unaware. Frank, taking charge, led them to a café; this, unlike Graham's discreet favourite place, was decorated in red with plastic surfaces – and there was a careless chip in the sugar. Frank, a men's outfitter, criticised Graham's clothes and when he learned of Graham's long-term mental health problems was extremely unsympathetic.

> Graham and his mother obviously have a close relationship and Graham is disturbed by its interruption through his mother's eager response to the flattery of this figure from her past. We not only see Frank through Graham's disapproving eye, but understand how Graham appears to the newly found friend of Vera Whittaker, especially after Graham discreetly withdraws to the lavatory so that his mother can explain to Frank about his problems of mental health. The two men are already in competition for Mrs Whittaker's attention.

SCENE 2 (PP. 20–2)   Visitors – the vicar and Frank Turnbull

The same: some time later, in late afternoon.

Graham describes the day's events. The vicar called for a donation to famine relief and received a verbal trouncing on his dress sense from Mrs Whittaker. Frank Turnbull then arrived and took Mrs Whittaker out in his car. Graham was not invited. He has been reading a magazine and fears that he is suffering from a recurrence of his anxiety symptoms, since he thinks he has heard someone knocking at the door – a delusion he has experienced in the past.

> The vicar's visit is a comic highlight in the play and shows Mrs Whittaker at her liveliest and most combative. It also shows something of the Whittakers' usual everyday life, with Graham in the role of domestic support. With the arrival of Frank, however, Graham's anxiety about this new relationship of his mother comes to the fore again; he is left alone in the house, fearing that some of the most frightening aspects of his illness are recurring.

SCENE 3 (PP. 22–4) A wedding announcement; is someone watching the house?

The same: another day, at night.

Mrs Whittaker and Frank have been to York. Graham's mother announced to him that she and Frank were to be married 'and the honeymoon is to be in Tenerife' (p. 23). In the same breath she tells Graham to take one of his 'tablets' (p. 23). Graham would be expected to move out to a hostel where he had spent some previous time. Graham cannot sleep and thinks someone is watching the house.

> Sympathy is divided here: Graham's anxiety about his mother's late-flowering romance causes him to worry, too, about his fragile health. The reader or viewer feels for him, but also probably recognises Mrs Whittaker's desperation in snatching at an unexpected chance of excitement and a different life away from Graham.

SCENE 4 (PP. 24–5) 'Community Caring'; Mr Turnbull's daughter arrives

The same: soon after the previous scene, in the evening.

Graham has been to a self-help therapy group at the Health Centre that morning. Mrs Whittaker's prospective marriage was discussed by those present, but Graham, who believes he has no problems himself, found the group's attitude unhelpful. Later in the day, when his mother and Turnbull had gone out for holiday purchases, Graham became aware that there really was someone knocking at the door, and was relieved that it had not been a figment of his imagination and the return of a symptom of his illness. The caller was Frank Turnbull's daughter.

> The account of the self-help group offers a satirical appraisal of this kind of therapy, even though Graham's description is apparently artless. Graham's appeal to his mother not to leave him is brushed aside and he is left to sit in the darkness so that 'they' cannot see him. He is finally persuaded that the knocking at the door that occurs is genuine and the arrival of Frank's daughter suggests that the plot of the short play is about to take a final turn.

SCENE 5 (PP. 25–7)   Turnbull unmasked; a row and a reconciliation

The same: a day or two later, at night.

Graham tells us that when Mrs Whittaker returned he broke the news to her that Frank Turnbull was a philanderer with an invalid wife. His daughter, who looked after her mother, had been obliged – not for the first time – to warn an unsuspecting victim that she was being misled. Mrs Whittaker, finally persuaded of the truth and understandably upset, behaved spitefully to Graham, saying that he was not normal and revealing that she knew he kept a store of pornographic magazines in his bedroom. However, by the following morning she seemed to have recovered her equanimity, and the play ends with Graham describing the resumption of their usual life together.

> Graham's triumph is complete. Frank is disgraced and his mother is pleased to revert to their former comfortable relationship – his health, too, has not deteriorated, as he had feared. Graham accepts his mother's wounding remarks about his sexual proclivities without offering any justification of himself. In the struggle for domination which occurs between Graham and his mother, honours end about even.

vis-à-vis (Fr. 'face to face') in relation to
spent a penny euphemism for 'went to the lavatory'
diddling her hands dabbling her hands in the water
the *Guardian* a liberal broadsheet daily newspaper
bifocals spectacles with lenses partly for near and partly for distant vision
piles haemorrhoids
she's wiring in she's eating enthusiastically
flares are anathema flared trousers are totally unacceptable
pulling your socks up making an effort
Featherbedding making things easy for someone
snotty snooty, snobbish
over the moon delighted
my whack my share
getting our skates on hurrying
spanking excellent, lively

he's your fancy man in embryo he's your prospective lover
the ghetto approach the segregated approach
Toodle pip goodbye
suited satisfied

BED AMONG THE LENTILS

SYNOPSIS

The narrator of *Bed Among the Lentils* is an unhappy woman, whose dissatisfaction with her life has made her turn to drink. Susan, married to a vicar, finds her religious belief shaky and questions her commitment to the Church of England, or Anglicanism. She doubts her husband Geoffrey's own convictions, seeing him as a self-seeking careerist. She is amused by his popularity with his parishioners and recognises that their devotion to him owes something to her own total failure to fulfil the traditional role of vicar's wife.

Susan gives wryly humorous accounts of various parish disasters in which she is involved. She provides an unappealing meal from tins and other convenience foods on the important occasion of a visit from the bishop, fails to help Geoffrey in his hopes of the bishop's support for promotion in the lunch-table discussion and, drunk by the end of the meal, spills milk over the bishop's gaiters. On another occasion, she quarrels with the parishioners during a flower-arranging session in the church, attacking the pretentious arrangement of Mrs Shrubsole, and finally collapsing in a state of intoxication on the altar steps. When she drinks up all the communion wine, Geoffrey is left in an awkward predicament at the morning service. Although it seems, at least at first, that Susan believes her drinking is a secret, it becomes clear as the narration proceeds that every one in the parish is aware of the situation, although it is not openly discussed.

The secret that Susan does keep from the parish throughout is the fact that she is having a sexual relationship with a Hindu shopkeeper, whom she meets first in nearby Leeds when she is searching for a new source of alcohol. She finds Ramesh Ramesh and his attitude to lovemaking very attractive; their uninhibited enjoyment contrasts with her unexciting sexual encounters with Geoffrey. She is interested, too, in the Hindu religion and draws fanciful parallels, to Ramesh's advantage, between Jesus and the Hindu shopkeeper. It is Ramesh who persuades Susan to tackle her alcoholism, although her husband believes that it is he who has done so. Geoffrey becomes something of a hero in Anglican circles, and his supposed success in helping Susan through her difficulties leads to his promotion. Reformed, perhaps temporarily, and parted from Ramesh, who has been to fetch his young bride from India and has moved to Preston, Susan ends her narrative on a defiant note.

SCENE 1 (PP. 30–1)   **Susan describes her day**

On a Sunday evening before Easter, in the vicarage kitchen.

Susan was late for communion and did not enjoy her husband's sermon on sex as an offering to God. The parish has learned that the bishop is to pay a visit. In the afternoon, avoiding Geoffrey's overtures, she said that she was delivering the parish magazine but in fact spent the afternoon in the car in a lay-by. She discusses her lack of interest in her role of vicar's wife and reveals that in the evening she went to the local off-licence to buy more sherry.

> Although Susan describes the day's events with a lively but wry humour, it is obvious that she is deeply unhappy. She describes her appearance in unattractive terms, is unsure of her faith in a Christian god, out of touch with her husband and values their sex life, ironically, at 10 pence – the offering that she puts into the church plate in response to his sermon. Susan resents, too, the parish duties that fall traditionally to a clergyman's wife. There is a first hint, in the failure of the woman in the off-licence to smile at Susan, that she drinks too much.

SCENE 2 (PP. 32–3)   **The bishop's visit; Susan and Ramesh**

After Easter. Afternoon, in the side-chapel.

The bishop's visit to the vicarage for lunch has not gone well. Susan has not responded satisfactorily to his enquiries about her commitment to the church and she has spilled tinned milk on his gaiters. Later, Susan tells us, she went into Leeds to see a handsome Asian shopkeeper, Ramesh Ramesh, whom she has discovered as a discreet source of alcohol. They sit in the back of his shop and talk about themselves and about Hinduism.

Susan provides an obviously unappealing meal for the bishop. There is **dramatic irony** in the fact that we know, although Susan apparently does not, that the bishop could hardly fail to notice Susan's intoxicated state. The visit to Ramesh Ramesh offers the chance for Susan to contrast Christianity and Hinduism. Although she feels she is not a believer, she is steeped in the traditional writings and ritual of the Church of England, as is clear through the many references and quotations from these sources which she includes in her narrative. She finds the Hindu shopkeeper much more attractive than her husband and is intrigued by the open eroticism of Hinduism.

SCENE 3 (PP. 33–7)   Flower arranging; a sexual encounter

Some time later. Morning, in the vicarage kitchen.

After describing how her life is not turning out as she would have wished, Susan gives an amusing account of an attempt at flower arranging with Mrs Shrubsole, Mrs Belcher and Miss Frobisher in the church. This ended when she fell, drunkenly attempting to demonstrate the shortcomings of an elaborate arrangement made by one of the parishioners. She was taken back to the vicarage to lie down whilst the ladies made a fuss of Geoffrey and generally humiliated her. Later in the day, she went to Leeds and, to her surprise, found herself making love with Ramesh, who had closed his shop early.

The hostility between Geoffrey's devoted parishioners and Susan is amusingly highlighted in the flower arranging sequence. Although Susan's humorous narrative attracts sympathy throughout, there is also a perhaps enjoyable sense of what a liability she must be to the parish – drunken and disaffected as she is. The sexual encounter with Ramesh has an air of inevitability about it, given Susan's account of previous visits.

SCENE 4 (PP. 37–8)   **Where is the communion wine?**

Summer. Afternoon, in the vestry.

Susan has drunk the communion wine and Geoffrey was unable to begin the service on the second Sunday after Trinity. Susan claims that she thought she had solved the problem by suggesting that he substitute cough mixture. Geoffrey was angry but nevertheless used it and no one noticed the difference. She describes how she missed Evensong and went to see Ramesh, whose uninhibited lovemaking upon the lentil sacks was a revelation to her.

> For Susan, the use of cough mixture for communion wine and the failure of any one to notice the substitution supports her lack of conviction about the significance of the rituals of the Church of England. She revels in the exoticism of making love with an attractive man from a different culture – on a bed made up of sacks of lentils.

SCENE 5 (PP. 38–41)   **Promotion for Geoffrey; reformation for Susan?**

Months later, in the vicarage drawing room.

Susan, looking unusually smart, describes how Ramesh persuaded her to give up drinking, although Geoffrey has taken the credit for it. His public pronouncements about the problems he believes they have come through together, as a triumph for his support and understanding, helped to forward his career plans. Susan's narrative ends with Geoffrey in line for a senior clerical appointment and Ramesh having moved to Preston after fetching his young wife from India. Though apparently a reformed character, Susan is as unconvinced as ever about the value of her role as a clergyman's wife – and she now has what she sees as the additional burden of regular attendance at tedious meetings of Alcoholics Anonymous.

> The irony in this tragicomedy bites deep when Geoffrey makes use – for career ambitions – of his belief that his has been the guiding force in rescuing Susan from alcoholism. Even in the confessional atmosphere of Alcoholics Anonymous, Susan keeps her secret about her life-enhancing relationship with Ramesh

Ramesh. She seems to bear no grudge against him for 'moving on' to marriage and a new shop in Preston and his attitude to life and ambition is contrasted with that of Geoffrey, whose fundamental insincerity has become increasingly obvious throughout the narration. That Susan does not feel that she will 'move on' suggests perhaps that her reformation is temporary and the play ends on a bleak note.

the Garden of Gethsemane the scene of the agony of Jesus Christ on the Mount of Olives, before he gives himself up for crucifixion
Almighty God, unto whom Collect, a short prayer from the Anglican communion service
bring home the bacon support the household financially, be the breadwinner
off-licence a shop selling alcoholic drink for consumption elsewhere
Meals on Wheels a voluntary organisation taking hot meals daily to the elderly and disabled
Carnation milk milk from a tin, as are the peaches
gaiters leather leggings, part of a bishop's formal attire
Mary Magdalen and the Nivea cream flippant reference to the New Testament account of Mary Magdalen's anointing of Jesus's feet with expensive oils (although Nivea is an inexpensive emollient cosmetic product)
instant instant coffee
getting up to all sorts the gods and goddesses are in various erotic postures
WI Women's Institute – a rural organisation for craftwork and social activities, established in Britain in 1915
Gert and Daisy stage names of Elsie and Doris Waters, a well-known music hall double act earlier in the twentieth century
The Wind in the Willows children's story by Kenneth Grahame (1859–1932) with animal characters and set in woodland and on the river bank (dramatised for the National Theatre, London, by Alan Bennett, 1990)
Bambi film (1942) by Walt Disney about a fawn
HAZFLOR a play upon the HAZCHEM sign, indicating dangerous chemicals
Duroglit 'Duraglit' is a polish for brass
Emily Brontë English novelist (1818–48), author of *Wuthering Heights*, who died tragically of tuberculosis at an early age
A turn-up for the books an unexpected piece of good fortune

BED AMONG LENTILS: GLOSSARY continued

Lighten our darkness ... Third Collect of Anglican evening prayer

take the bull by the horns face a difficult situation bravely

the road to Damascus St Paul experienced a vision of Jesus on his way to Damascus – this determined the future course of his life

young upwardly mobile parsons pun on young, upwardly mobile persons, or YUPPIES, a feature of 1980s life

rural dean the head of a section of country clergy

A LADY OF LETTERS

SYNOPSIS

Miss Irene Ruddock is a lonely, middle-aged woman who has lived on her own in the family house since her mother died. She fills in some of her many spare hours with letter writing, usually consisting of complaints and suggestions to businesses, local authorities and her MP. In her mother's day, every one in the street knew every one else; nowadays, occupants change frequently and Miss Ruddock does not know personally any of her neighbours, although she keeps a keen eye upon them from her front bay window.

She suffers from nervous problems, although she has no confidence in the ability of the doctors at her local practice to treat her mental health difficulties.

After accounts of fairly harmless – even, occasionally, public-spirited – letter writing, a less innocuous side to her hobby is revealed. She has written anonymous letters accusing various local people of imaginary crimes and misdemeanours. The recently arrived young couple who live opposite have attracted her attention: she believes they neglect their sickly child. When the police arrive, it is clear that she has been writing libellous letters again – on this occasion about the young couple, whose child, we learn, has just died from leukaemia.

She is given a suspended sentence after having broken a previous court ruling, and two social workers try to help her to 'widen her horizons', much to her contempt. She is now obsessed with a supposed affair between the local policeman and a housewife along the road and, inevitably, finds herself in prison for yet more letter writing.

The play has a surprise ending, since it turns out that prison offers redemption to Miss Ruddock. She learns new skills and actually communicates with the other inmates, whose lives have often suffered tragedies undreamed of by 'Irene', as she is now called, in contrast to the imaginary petty intrigues in which she has been involved at home. A happy ending, then, with Irene even prepared to take a job when she leaves prison.

SCENE 1 (PP. 44–5)   A funeral service and some correspondence

Afternoon, in a bay-windowed room.

Miss Ruddock describes the funeral service (for Miss Pringle, a casual acquaintance) that she has recently attended. We soon learn that she takes it upon herself to write letters of complaint upon the slightest pretext. She has written to the director of the local crematorium about hearse drivers smoking outside the chapel, and is pleased that this has resulted in a brief correspondence. New neighbours have moved in opposite her house – a young couple with a child, who – in Miss Ruddock's view – looks grubby.

Miss Ruddock's need to fill in her lonely days is revealed by her making an outing to the crematorium for the funeral of someone she has met occasionally at a local bus stop. Her letter writing serves the same purpose of finding an activity to fill in the time that hangs heavily on her hands, although she believes that she is performing a useful and necessary service. She keeps an eye on the neighbours from her bay window.

SCENE 2 (PP. 45–6)   More correspondence and worrying new neighbours

Some time later. Late afternoon or evening, in the same room.

Miss Ruddock tells us more about a wide range of letters she has written which have brought gratifying results. Her fountain pen is a prized last present from her late, much loved mother. She has noticed a bruise on the arm of the child living opposite and has heard it crying.

Miss Ruddock is an accomplished communicator, it appears, with no outlet for her talents except through her obsessive letter writing.

Her complaints about 'dog dirt' and a broken paving slab can be described as public spirited, but other correspondence is less praiseworthy.

SCENE 3 (PP. 46–7)   **Miss Ruddock's views on prison; a hair in the sausages; more worries about the new neighbours**

A week or two have passed. It is afternoon.

Miss Ruddock, who has been reading her newspaper, says that life in prison is too easy and leads to more crime. She writes regularly to her MP about crime, it appears, most recently about the undesirability of employing policemen who wear spectacles. She has just written to a sausage manufacturer about a hair she has found in their product that morning. Miss Ruddock is confirmed in her poor opinion of the young couple opposite: they are always out at night and no baby-sitter arrives.

Miss Ruddock is clearly becoming very concerned about the young couple opposite and their child. She speculates on their circumstances, although there is apparently no question of her getting to know them or even of speaking to them.

SCENE 4 (PP. 47–8)   **A visit to the doctor**

Dusk, on a different day. Miss Ruddock is at the window.

Miss Ruddock tells us that her mother knew every one in the street and regrets the loss of community spirit . Worried about the child opposite, she has been to the doctor (as usual, an unfamiliar figure to her in the large group practice) to tell him about her anxiety. We learn that she has problems with mental health – she 'gets upset' – and the doctor, referring to her medical notes, dismisses her fears as he writes out a new prescription. She has no confidence in this medication and decides to 'put it down the toilet'.

Miss Ruddock miss the neighbourliness which her mother appreciated but is unable to see that she is contributing to this loss by failing to communicate directly with those around her, although she observes closely through her bay window all that goes on.

SCENE 5 (PP. 48–9)   The vicar calls; Miss Ruddock is arrested

Some time later. A bare background.

Miss Ruddock continues her narrative, apparently at the police station. The doctor, she tells us, had asked the vicar to call on her but she cut short his evangelical efforts by telling him she was an atheist. Then she reveals that the police have called about anonymous letters she had been writing concerning the couple opposite, and we learn that Miss Ruddock has not previously been telling the whole truth about her apparently harmless letter writing. She has already been bound over to keep the peace by a magistrates' court after accusing the chemist's wife of being a prostitute and the crossing warden of being a child molester. The child opposite had not been neglected but had been ill with leukaemia, from which it had just died in hospital, and the police arrived to arrest her.

After the humour of Miss Ruddock's attack upon the unfortunate vicar, the narrative takes a sombre turn, as her propensity for meddling is shown to have criminal implications. She records the death from leukaemia of the child she had wrongly supposed to be ill-treated without any expression of regret for her mistake.

SCENE 6 (PP. 50–1)   Miss Ruddock has two social workers to help her

A week or more later. Daytime, at home.

Miss Ruddock tells us she has been given a suspended sentence for her malicious letter writing and now has two social workers, whom she does not appreciate, to help her. One of them insists on calling her Irene, much to her annoyance. They make various suggestions, none of which Miss Ruddock finds useful. She is now worried about a local police constable who is, she claims, spending too much time with a housewife further down the road.

Miss Ruddock is not able to see off the social workers allocated to her as she did the vicar, but this is another scene of considerable humour, in which some of the approaches of the social services are satirised. There is an ominous touch to her new interest — in the fancied affair between the local policeman and a neighbour.

SCENE 7 (PP. 51–3)   **Prison and regeneration**

Some while afterwards. An institutional setting.

Miss Ruddock has undergone a dramatic change: she is in prison, having written one letter too many. But, surprisingly, she is having a wonderful time. Wearing an unfamiliar tracksuit and happy to be 'Irene' to all the other inmates, she is thoroughly enjoying the prison classes and even looking forward to a job when she is released. She finds she has many skills, not least a most neglected one – the ability to lend a friendly ear to others' troubles. Some inmates have experienced harrowing circumstances in their lives and Miss Ruddock weighs their difficulties against her own – 'You don't know you're born I think' (p.51). Unlikely though it may be to find fulfilment in prison, Miss Ruddock acknowledges her happiness.

The play has an unexpectedly buoyant ending. The prison sentence is not unsurprising, given what has gone before, but 'Irene's' blossoming provides a cheerful resolution to her sad story. Her letter writing for the illiterate is, at last, really useful; the enforced companionship with her sister inmates, as well as the tragedies in some of their lives, help her towards a positive attitude to her own life.

tab ends cigarette ends
Platignum the brand name of Miss Ruddock's fountain pen
Awayday one-day reduced price railway ticket
lady in waiting traditional title for a member of HRH the Queen's personal staff
Basildon Bond a brand of writing paper
lollipop man crossing warden who sees children across the road
shantung natural silk
SS (German) Schutz-Staffel – Nazi special police force, notorious for their brutality

SYNOPSIS

Lesley, an actress in her early thirties, tells the story of her 'big chance' – in a film role playing the leading female character. Lesley prides herself on her breadth of interests and her willingness to acquire further skills. She reads self-help books on personality development and believes she is a lively conversationalist with a sympathetic manner. She also believes that she is sophisticated, although she easily succumbs to the various men in her narration who persuade her to spend the night with them.

Lesley has previously had a non-speaking role in *Tess*, a prestigious film directed by Roman Polanski, and thinks herself to be well-equipped for the role of Travis, which she is offered through a mistaken belief that she can water-ski. The film turns out eventually to be a degrading sex and violence story, which is to be released on video, although the naïve Lesley never realises the true nature of the film in which she is involved. She sees herself as a serious actress and constantly offers helpful hints to the director, Gunther – through his assistant, Simon – as to ways in which Travis's character could be developed.

Lesley spends a night each with various members of the filming team, and finally with the director, Gunther, although she is not included in other social activities. Lesley's narration ends with her well satisfied with her work in the film, although she lost even the one line she had, and was persuaded to appear in a nude scene. Her plans for the future include the possibility of some different money-making schemes and, of course, further development of her personality.

SCENE 1 (PP. 56–8)   **An audition is arranged for a film role for Lesley**

Morning, Lesley's flat.

Lesley has recently finished making a film, she tells us. She describes a walk-on part she once played in a TV serial, explains her dedication to her work and how she prides herself on being a professional. Going back to the just-completed film and the means by which she was given the role, she describes how at a party she met Spud, a man who said he was 'on the production side' of film work. He arranged an audition for Lesley the next morning and offered her a bed nearby for the night. We are left to conclude that Lesley slept with him and that she was disappointed when she assessed from his vest and his tattoo that he was an electrician.

It is already obvious that Lesley is a silly, self-deluding woman, whose estimation of her gifts we are not likely to accept. We also suspect that she is used to exchanging favours by going to bed with any man who can help her: in spite of her slick protestations, it is clear that Lesley expected to have to sleep with Spud after he arranged an audition for her. Her judgement of his status from intimate observation suggests that she is well-versed in these matters, too.

SCENE 2 (PP. 58–60)   The audition

A few weeks earlier, after the audition. Afternoon, Lesley's flat.

Lesley is very pleased with her performance at the audition, which was for the role of a character called Travis. The first requirement was for Lesley to strip to her underclothes, since in the film Travis spends most of her time sunbathing on board a yacht. Lesley was quite happy to undress, and this part of the audition was successful. Lesley then re-enacts the discussion which followed, with her attempts at bright conversation and all the suggestions she made for developing the part of Travis. Simon, who interviewed her, said that they needed someone who could water-ski and perhaps play chess. Lesley ends the scene surprised that she has heard no more.

It is no surprise to the reader that Lesley has heard no more, since we guess, not least from the account of the interrupted telephone call, that Simon was astonished by her pretentiousness. There is some pathos, as well as humour, in Lesley's dependence on an American self-help guide to success in interviews.

SCENE 3 (PP. 60–2)   Lesley has the part

A week or so later. Morning, a dismal dressing-room on the film set at Lee-on-Solent.

Lesley tells us that, at the last minute, she was telephoned by Nigel, the director's assistant, and offered the part of Travis. So far she has not been on the set. It appears that Nigel thought that Lesley could water-ski and this is essential to the script. A local girl has been doubling for her. The make-up and wardrobe man, Scott, was disagreeable to her from the first, but last evening she met Terry, a cameraman. They went out for the evening and later Lesley shared his room, which she says was nicer than hers.

We guess that Nigel telephoned the wrong girl and that Lesley was given the part of Travis by mistake, since water-skiing ability was essential. Her failure to see that she is not the sparkling success she believes herself to be is the source of considerable comedy. She is easy prey for Terry, the cameraman.

SCENE 4 (PP. 63–5)   **Lesley takes her clothes off; another evening out**

Later, during filming. Evening, Lesley's hotel room.

Lesley describes a day's filming which she spent pretending to sunbathe on the deck of the yacht, whilst the actors playing her elderly lover and his business associate were the focal point. She describes how Nigel persuaded her to take off first her bikini top and then the bottom. Lesley persisted with her ideas for building up Travis's film personality and was humoured a little by Nigel and Gunther (the real director). In the evening, Lesley discovered that every one had gone out again – leaving her behind – to supper at the restaurant run by her water-skiing stand-in. Eventually, in the bar, she met Kenny, the animal handler on the film. She went to his room to see the animals and stayed the night.

Nigel manages to persuade Lesley to take off her clothes and we guess that it has been decided that her contribution to the film will be to provide nude scenes. Some explanation for her promiscuity is offered by her evident loneliness.

SCENE 5 (PP. 65–7)   **The end of the film; Lesley looks to the future**

After the end of filming. Dusk, Lesley's flat.

Lesley describes the climax of the film, when she was required to kill her lover with a harpoon gun. She lost what was to have been her 'big' line about having a headache, which she explains to her own satisfaction. Right up until the end, she has been making suggestions which she believes will assist the director, and is prepared to engage in sexual intercourse on screen. On the last night she went to bed with Gunther and learned that the film would come out on video in Germany and perhaps Turkey. Lesley ends this scene by describing her plans to take up various random interests and further develop her personality.

We understand that Lesley's 'big chance' has actually consisted of a small role in a low grade film involving violence and nudity. Her attempts at self-improvement go unnoticed: she is in demand only for sexual favours.

Crossroads television serial, 1964–88, set in a motel
Are you on cans are you in contact with the director – through your earphones
Woman in a Musquash Coat identification of an 'extra' in filming
Richard Attenborough British film actor and director
the rat race the competitive world
in the pipeline under way, already begun
Tess film version of the novel *Tess of the d'Urbervilles*, by Thomas Hardy (1840–1928)
Ciao (Italian, informal) goodbye
local sub-aqua local water sports centre
p.o.v. point of view
making continuity a bugger (slang, impolite) making continuity awkward
Emily Brontë English novelist (1818–48), author of *Wuthering Heights,* who died tragically of tuberculosis at an early age
knockers (slang, impolite) breasts
Elbow the bikini bottom get rid of the bottom half of the swim suit
a hair in the gate fault in the film caused by a blemish on the lens
West Germany between 1949 and 1990 Germany was divided in two, the larger part being known as 'West Germany'

SOLDIERING ON

SYNOPSIS

Muriel Carpenter is 'a brisk, sensible woman in her late fifties' (p. 70). At the beginning of her narrative the funeral of her husband, Ralph, has just taken place, and she has been left in excellent financial circumstances. A conventional middle-class woman, she has wide experience of running a house and acting as hostess for her husband, who has served in the army and, at the time of his death, was a prosperous business executive. Muriel's response to her bereavement is to control her grief and 'soldier on', as she has done all her life.

Her daughter, Margaret, has long-term mental health problems and after her father's funeral, which she does not attend, believes that the police are about to arrest her. Muriel looks after her patiently, but it is clear that she dotes upon her son, Giles, who is married to Pippa and has two children, Crispin and Lucy.

Giles is the cause of his mother's financial downfall, as he persuades her into unwise investment projects, which leave her and many others ruined. Her comfortable home and elegant possessions are sold to set against the debts Giles has incurred on her behalf (his own position is secure), and she is reduced to living in penury in a seaside bed-sitting room. Still she will not hear a word against Giles, but is sad that he seldom makes contact with her and that she has lost touch with her grandchildren.

Meanwhile, an explanation for Margaret's mental illness is gradually revealed: Ralph abused his daughter, it is discovered by the despised National Health Service psychiatrist who treats Margaret when her mother can no longer pay for a private nursing home. She begins to respond to treatment and is 'just like a normal girl' towards the end of the narrative.

Poor Muriel, penniless, cut off from her grandchildren and unable to make use of her obvious energy and skills, nevertheless refuses to accept that she is a tragic figure. As always, she makes the best of things, although her prospects are unenviable.

SCENE 1 (PP. 70–1)   A funeral

The day after her husband's funeral. Afternoon, a room in the comfortable house of Muriel, a middle-class woman in her late fifties.

Her husband, Ralph, has died and she recounts the events of the previous day, when the funeral took place. The range of Ralph's connections was wide: mourners were present who knew him through work, the army, the

Church, sport and various charities. We learn that Muriel's son, Giles, and his wife and children were a great help. Her daughter, Margaret, had kept out of the way but appeared after the mourners had left. She did not seem to understand about her father's death and Muriel gave her a tablet to calm her.

> Muriel is in control of her grief. She is an accomplished hostess who, even in an emotional state after the funeral service, puts the needs of her guests first. We learn that her daughter, Margaret, has mental health problems as she is confused about her father's death and Muriel gives her a sedative.

SCENE 2 (PP. 72–4)   **Ralph's personal possessions; Giles's advice**

Some days later. Evening, Muriel is in an armchair.

Muriel tells us about disposing of her husband's personal possessions. Following what she knew was Ralph's advice in any new situation, she tried to find out what help and advice was available to the newly bereaved. There was little, but every one told her not to take any big decisions. In spite of this, she allowed Giles to persuade her, after a lavish lunch out, to let him invest money on her behalf. Ralph had left her very well off. Giles also took away some valuable items to hide, in order to circumvent estate duty. Margaret, who we learn has long-term health problems, has suffered from the delusion that the police were coming to take her away. With the help of Mabel, her trusted housekeeper, Muriel manages to get her daughter upstairs to bed and gives her her medication.

> Muriel speaks very differently of her son, Giles, obviously her favourite, and her daughter Muriel. Although she has her doubts about the wisdom of Giles's investment plans, she is easily persuaded to take his advice. Giles's behaviour in taking advantage of his mother's drowsiness after a heavy lunch begins to cause suspicion about his integrity, as does his removal of valuable items from the family home in order to cheat the estate assessors. However, it is clear that, in his mother's eyes, Giles can do no wrong. Her attitude to her sick daughter, Margaret, is different and seems to lack any tenderness, as Muriel speaks of 'manhandling' her upstairs. Margaret's illness requires her to be supervised at all times,

it appears, since Mabel has to 'hold the fort' whilst Muriel goes out to lunch with Giles, and a holiday abroad would be a possibility only if Margaret were to be hospitalised.

SCENE 3 (PP. 74–6) **No private care for Margaret; no capital for Muriel to start a small business**

Some days or weeks later. Afternoon.

Muriel has been writing letters. Margaret has had to go into hospital. Previously she has been looked after under what Muriel considers ideal conditions in a private nursing home. Now, Muriel is upset that, because Giles has told her she cannot afford it, Margaret is in an overcrowded National Health Service psychiatric hospital where the facilities are very poor. Muriel is writing letters to her many contacts to try to raise money for mental health resources. Mental health is a mystery, she says. Giles has told her, puzzlingly, that there is no capital available for her to start a small business.

Although Muriel does not recognise it, Giles is obviously untrustworthy and incompetent over money matters; his mother's financial situation begins to look grave. She obviously has the skills and energy to run a small business, but even that is ruled out by Giles.

SCENE 4 (PP. 76–7) **Financial ruin; Margaret's health shows signs of improvement**

Some weeks later. Afternoon, Muriel is in a bare room.

Giles's investment plans have turned out disastrously: many people have been financially ruined, including Muriel, although Giles's own property is secure. Muriel's house and contents have had to be sold at auction, but she tells us she finds she does not much care for possessions. She makes excuses for Giles. At an interview with her daughter's young psychiatrist, Muriel learns that Margaret is making a little progress. The psychiatrist asks Muriel about Margaret's relationship with her father, when she was a child.

Giles is proved to be a scoundrel, although Muriel cannot see it and still defends him. Hints are accumulating that Ralph may have abused his daughter: Muriel seems to have become aware of this possibility, as is shown when she says 'Bloody psychiatrist'.

SCENE 5 (PP. 77–9)   'Soldiering on'

A month or more later. Evening.

Muriel makes the best of things living on a tiny income in an off-season 'holiday flatlet' in Hunstanton. Margaret is much better and there is some likelihood of a normal life for her. She and Muriel have been able to talk about Ralph and what Muriel calls 'etc'. Margaret does not blame her father any more for his abuse of her, and Muriel decides that she feels sorry for him. She is equally unjudgemental about Giles and his despicable conduct. She has discovered the comforts of the television and enjoys listening to tapes she borrows from the library. Muriel concludes her narrative by denying that her story is tragic, or that she is a tragic woman.

Although Muriel has suffered financial disaster on a dramatic scale, she is able to respond with fortitude – 'soldiering on' (p. 78) as she puts it. There is the prospect of a happier relationship in the future with her daughter, whose mental health problems seem to have been competently dealt with by the National Health Service. The appalling Giles seems to have severed relations with the mother he has ruined, and she misses the grandmotherly duties she had looked forward to with his children. However, she makes the best of her limited opportunities in Hunstanton, chats with strangers in the town, takes advantage of the consolations of the 'telly box' (p. 79), and refuses to admit that the narrative she has related is a tragedy.

beef en croute beef cooked in pastry
Massey-Ferguson a tractor-making firm for which Ralph presumably worked
light the blue touch paper and retire light the firework and stand back – here, introduce two people and hope they will get on together
Household Brigade a brigade from the elite troops who normally guard the sovereign
chocker (slang) full – probably from 'chock-a-block'
blub (slang) weep – from 'blubber'
gone into floods gone into floods of tears

Hawes and Curtis tailors of Jermyn Street, London SW1
a little zizz a little sleep, nap
liquidity problem lack of readily accessible funds
'the index is going down' quoted share prices on the Stock Market are falling
the revenue tax officials
'drag our brogues' usually 'drag our feet' – postpone doing something
Nikolaus Pevsner 1902–83 – well-known writer on art and architecture
qua **building, not displeasing** as a building, attractive enough architecturally
National Trust trust for the preservation of places of historic interest or
national beauty, founded 1895
different ball game US cliché for a marked change from something familiar
NUPE National Union of Public Employees
A propos on the subject (of)
'All hands to the pumps' (nautical) every one needs to respond to the
emergency
nouvelle *nouvelle cuisine* (French) an elaborate cooking style of the 1980s,
offering very small portions
Lay not up for yourself treasures on earth see the Bible, Matthew 6:28
Sloane Street fashionable address of Giles's home in London
cossy (slang, originally Australian) swimming costume
The Lady monthly magazine catering for conventional middle-class women
Meals on Wheels a public service whereby meals are delivered (by
volunteers) to the homes of the elderly or disabled
2 i/c second in command
orphans of the storm traditional reference to a desperate situation, perhaps
referring to a once familiar painting or melodrama
young man in orange follower of so-called 'Hare Krishna' cult
precinct here, shopping area
prep. (school slang) preparation
up to pres. up to the present
Peter Pan here, the statue in Kensington Gardens, London, of a character,
the perpetually young Peter Pan, from Sir James Barrie's 1904 play of the
same name for children
Science Museum in Kensington, London

SYNOPSIS

Doris, the narrator, is a frail seventy-five year old widow. As the play begins, she is sitting on a low chair, to which she has struggled after a fall. Although her weekly home help, Zulema, has strictly forbidden Doris to do any cleaning, on pain of being sent to the local old people's home, Stafford House, Doris has wilfully tried to dust the top of a wedding photograph of herself and her late husband, Wilfred. The photograph has fallen, its glass broken; Doris, too, has fallen and injured her leg, which is numb.

Doris is very fussy about her house and garden, and does not trust Zulema to clean properly, a view which is justified when, from her position now on the floor, she spots an old biscuit – a cream cracker – under the settee. She manages to get to the front door but is unable to reach to open it. She reminisces throughout about her married life with Wilfred, his unfulfilled ambitions for various hobbies, and about their failure to have children – her only baby was stillborn. Back in her living room, still with the wedding photograph beside her, she finds that numbness has spread to her other leg. She anticipates life in Stafford House, which she feels she could not tolerate; she imagines a relentless cheerfulness and a smell of urine. When help arrives – in the form of the local policeman, who knocks at the door to ask if everything is all right – she makes the decision to pretend that nothing is wrong and to send him away. No one else will call and she has decided to die, rather than go to Stafford House.

Her final reminiscences, as she becomes fainter and her mind begins to wander, are of happier days – her early married life, and her childhood bedtimes.

SCENE 1 (PP. 82–4)   **Doris has had a fall, attempting to do the forbidden dusting**

Morning, the living room of Doris's semi-detached house.

She is sitting on a low chair: Doris has fallen and hurt her leg, she tells us, as she tries to rub the numbness away. Her home help, Zulema, who has just finished her weekly visit, has told her she must not attempt housework. However, Doris is unimpressed by Zulema's cleaning standards and she fell after clambering onto a stool in order to dust the top of a framed wedding photograph of herself and her late husband, Wilfred. The photograph fell too, and the glass is cracked. She is not in good health, we gather, since she is forbidden housework, suffers from dizzy spells and has a pacemaker; her worst fear is that she will have to go into a local old people's home, Stafford House. She worries about the gate banging and about leaves from next door on the path of her front garden. Her leg is still numb, but she decides to try to get up to make a cup of tea.

Zulema sounds very sensible in her warnings to Doris, but already we guess that Doris is somewhat obsessively concerned about the level of cleanliness that Zulema is maintaining in her house. Her concern extends to the garden and the leaves that have blown in untidily from next door. Her late husband Wilfred it seems won a rare battle over the garden and was allowed a small evergreen bush instead of the 'hygienic' concrete that Doris would have preferred. She keeps the photograph with its cracked glass with her throughout the play, and often addresses her husband in the wedding picture.

SCENE 2 (PP. 84–6)   The cream cracker; life with Wilfred

Later that day, the living room.

Doris is sitting on the floor, leaning against the wall: Doris's leg gave way when she tried to get up and she is now on the floor, from which vantage point she is able to see 'a cream cracker under the settee' (p. 84), evidence of Zulema's superficial cleaning. She talks about Wilfred, describing hobbies she has apparently discouraged him from taking up in the past, fearing mess and 'muck'. She would have allowed him a small dog, in spite of 'all the little hairs' (p. 85), but he did not get one. When someone comes through the gate, she thinks help might be coming, but it turns out to be only a child who urinates in her front garden, to Doris's disgust. She decides to try to get to the front door, which she might be able to open in order to get help.

We are given a picture of the married life of Doris and her husband: Wilfred had many ideas for hobbies and enterprises which never materialised – we guess at least partly because of his wife's disapproval. They would have liked children: 'a kiddy'd've solved all that' (p. 85), Doris says, in relation to her husband's thwarted enthusiasms.

SCENE 3 (PP. 86–8)   **Doris is on the floor in the hall, where the perambulator once stood**

Later, in the hall. Doris is now on the floor with her back to the front door.

Doris is reminded of the big perambulator which had stood in the hall and which Wilfred had bought when she was pregnant in the early days of their marriage. She cannot reach the lock to open the door and is dozing when a leaflet is pushed through the letter-box. Her one child was apparently stillborn. The midwife wrapped him up in newspaper, Doris remembers resentfully, and she thinks how different life might be now if she had had children and grandchildren. Her only callers are people she does not know, like the Evangelists she mocks. Her other leg begins to feel numb, too.

A healthy baby might have changed the lives of Doris and Wilfred, perhaps; Doris would have been less obsessed with dust and cleaning and Wilfred would have found a new interest. Doris seems to contradict what she said in the previous scene when she suggests, 'I don't think Wilfred minded' (p. 88), and we wonder whether the prospect of fatherhood really was 'Just a craze' (p. 88), or whether his apparent acceptance of the loss of the baby was intended to comfort her.

SCENE 4 (PP. 88–91)   **Doris makes a decision**

Evening, the living room again. Doris is propped up against the sofa.

She talks about clothes she has had made for herself and about all the baby's things she has put away, unused, upstairs. She eats the cream cracker from under the settee. She imagines what she considers would be a nightmare life in the old people's home to which she realises she will be directed, now she has had a bad fall on her own.

Her narration becomes vaguer, as she reminisces about happy times of her early married days in the past, which she believes was a golden age of cleanliness and friendliness. When the local policeman knocks at the door, to enquire if she is all right, she has decided that, rather than go to Stafford House, she will let nature take its course. She calls out to the policeman, pretending all is well. She speaks as though to Wilfred, then voices her final thoughts, which go back to her memory of an idyllic childhood bedtime, when she was washed and in a clean nightdress, ready to be tucked up for the night.

Doris's savage description of life at Stafford House is highly entertaining and probably quite unfair. But this is Doris's view of what her future will be, and justifies her almost heroic decision to die. It is clear to the very end of the play that Doris's concept of happiness is closely bound up with cleanliness, which she measures against a childhood recollection of perfection – warm fire, washed child, clean nightdress and a hot water bottle waiting in her bed.

Ewbank brand name of a carpet sweeper
Pull your horns in be less ambitious
swill the flags wash the stone floor
buffet (dialect) stool
We're cracked also (slang) 'we're crazy'
sneck (dialect) catch, gate fastening
you'll be on the carpet you'll be reprimanded
spending a penny urinating
them frame things walking supports, such as a Zimmer frame
jump the gun act prematurely
Braying on the door (dialect) banging, knocking on the door
stink here, a mild expletive
costume suit
side the pots (dialect) clear the table
My Alice Blue Gown popular song of the early twentieth century

PART THREE

CRITICAL APPROACHES

THE TITLE

talking head: a person appearing on television who merely talks, either directly to the audience, or in discussion with others in the studio, rather than presenting information in a more visually entertaining manner. Used in the world of the media since the 1970s (*The Shorter Slang Dictionary*, Routledge, 1994)

It would seem from the definition above that a 'talking head' is a synonym for boredom in a television age of dazzling – sometimes bewildering – visual entertainment. This is a challenge that Alan Bennett confronts head on.

First, he capitalises on the intimacy that the television screen can offer to drama; the long camera 'takes' draw us into the **narrator's** world in a way that the rapid change of angle and scene – familiar in much of what is presented on television – cannot. Our concentration is steadily invited, rather than fought for by multi-angled images.

Secondly, his characters' narratives are riveting rather than boring, because – just as he has been said to have made 'gossip into drama', so he has made an art-form out of the tedious. Recognisable as firmly based on real life as these dialogues are, they are nothing like **verbatim** transcripts of conversations, but are artfully contrived to convey the humour and pathos of his characters' situations. Alan Bennett wrote another similarly constructed short play which preceded *Talking Heads*, called *A Woman of No Importance*, in which the actress who later played Miss Ruddock took the role of a Miss Schofield. In the 'Introduction' to *Objects of Affection and Other Plays for TV* (BBC, 1982), which included *A Woman of No Importance*, he wrote of that narrator that 'to have her in full close-up, retailing in unremitting detail how, for instance, she borrowed the salt in the canteen, takes one beyond, I hope, tedium'. He thought that the more one knew about his characters, the more they could be understood. They each justify a demand for our attention to their situation in a world which is not right for them.

THE CHARACTERS

GRAHAM IN A CHIP IN THE SUGAR

We learn gradually from the **narrator**, 'mild middle-aged' (p. 16) Graham, that he has long-term problems of mental health and has to take 'tablets', especially at times of stress. He has lived in a hostel and has worked intermittently at therapeutic crafts such as flower- and soft toy-making. But for a long time he has lived at home with his elderly widowed mother, in effect running the household; although, as Alan Bennett says in his 'Introduction', Graham 'would not accept that he is married to his mother', their relationship does have an established domestic quality about it. Mrs Whittaker is pleased when she is taken for Graham's wife by someone in the street; she skittishly refers to him later as her 'boyfriend' and likes to walk arm in arm with him. Although the realisation that he could even for a moment be taken for his mother's husband disturbs Graham, their interdependence seems to go deep: they enjoy little outings and Graham teaches his mother the liberal views which he has acquired from the *Guardian* newspaper. Like her son, she appreciates the niceties of different architectural styles and the 'classy' little cafés that he selects for their minor indulgences at tea and coffee times.

So Graham is greatly disturbed that his mother should be easily won away from him by an admirer from a past so distant it is even 'pre-Dad'. This friend from the past, Frank Turnbull, is a vulgar little man, flashily dressed and with the views of the more reactionary tabloid newspapers. Graham is particularly wounded that his mother so readily rejects his ideas and becomes a mouthpiece for Frank. The philistine and illiberal Frank has no time for Graham, and no sympathy with his illness, saying that he thinks 'the solution to mental illness is hard physical work' (p. 19). Graham becomes increasingly upset by his mother's defection and what seems like her collusion with a man who despises her son.

Soon there is a wedding in the offing and the expulsion of Graham from his mother's home is to follow 'You were happy in the hostel. You rubbed shoulders with all sorts' (p. 23). But the romance ends with an explanation – off stage – from Frank's daughter. She is someone who has been watching the house and Graham believes her to be a figment of his imagination, or a symptom of a relapse into a serious state of illness.

Frank is an aged Don Juan, it appears, who has taken advantage of other women before and is married to an invalid wife. Mrs Whittaker is disappointed in her bid to escape from her son, whom she describes in an outburst as 'not normal'. She soon recovers her dignity, however, as domestic harmony is – more or less – restored. 'Harmony' is not perhaps quite the right word, since the relationship between Graham and Mrs Whittaker involves them in a constant low-level struggle for control, the object of which is to avoid allowing either to 'get it over' the other (i.e. take up a superior position). The narrative opens with Graham's account of an early morning conversation the day after Mrs Whittaker's (perhaps symbolic) fall and flirtatious encounter with Frank. Mrs Whittaker reassures Graham: 'I think the world of you.' He reciprocates and during the reconciliation she challenges his tea-making skills: 'This tea looks strong' but Graham reasserts his authority with: 'Give me your teeth. I'll swill them' (p. 16). This undercurrent develops throughout the play, with Graham commenting – not always to his mother – on those faults and physical failings which he knows make her dependent upon him: her vanity, her poor memory, her 'unpredictable bowels'. Mrs Whittaker, who exhibits an almost adolescent fecklessness in her unexpected fling with Frank, abandons all the values she supposedly shares with Graham and adopts Frank's views and style wholesale. Just as easily she resumes Graham's interests at the play's conclusion: 'We like old buildings, don't we, you and me?' (p.27) she says, as if nothing had happened, when they prepare for one of their familiar outings.

Although Mrs Whittaker is contrite and obviously prepared to make the best of her life with Graham again, her attempt at escape shows perhaps how trapped she had felt in her life with her son. Her lack of control on the previous night, when Graham had told her about Frank's perfidy, reveals cruelly to Graham how she thinks about him: 'How can you understand, you, you're not normal?' (p. 26). And, finally, she re-establishes her position, supposing that he might think that his judgement over Frank had been superior to hers, shouting: 'You think you've got it over me, Graham Whittaker. Well, you haven't, I've got it over you … I know the kind of magazines you read.' 'Chess …' 'They never are chess. Chess with no clothes on. Chess in their birthday suits. That kind of chess. Chess men' (p. 26). He can only counter, reminding her of her weak memory, 'Go to bed. And turn your blanket off.' The play ends with much the same kind of balance of power with which it opened. Mrs Whittaker, still lively, wins sympathy, although we never see her, and we understand how she is attracted to the vulgar but optimistic and 'natty' Frank: he is such a contrast to the timid Graham, far from 'natty' with his clammy feet, plastic mac and flared trousers, and with his constant pessimistic reminders of her growing frailties. Graham explains at the beginning of the monologue that his mother is not actually disabled, although she likes the added comfort of 'disabled' facilities in the public lavatories, but that 'her memory's bad'. Graham often has to tell her how old she is, for instance, and by the following day she has forgotten her fall in the street, although it has made her side feel stiff. And yet she says accusingly to Graham, after Frank's trickery has been revealed: 'That's another thing. I remembered with him. I don't remember with you' (p. 26). The implication is that her poor memory is a defensive weapon against the disappointing past which has centred on Graham. Frank was 'pre-Dad' and put her in touch again with the carefree Vera of her youthful days, days which she seems to have been trying to recapture. In any case, her relationship with the forceful, if insensitive and insincere, Frank has caused her memory to revive with her hopes.

The vulnerable narrator, however, Graham himself, is the central focus of pity and concern. As Alan Bennett writes in his 'Introduction', he is – like other narrators in *Talking Heads* – 'artless' in what he says, and it is in his re-enacted reports of conversation that most of the comedy of the monologue lies, although perhaps Graham is not unaware of the irony in some of the passages. He is surely aware of his mother's lack of even his own degree of sophistication when he records her saying: 'I like new experiences in eating. I had a pizza once, didn't I, Graham?' (p.18) and 'Graham's quite refined. He often has a dry sherry' (p. 19). But he is apparently unaware that he reveals his own limitations gradually to us. He seems to be artless, for instance, when he accepts the praise offered in a cliché by Dr Chaudhury, appreciating Graham's attempts to widen his mother's interests: 'The best way to avoid a broken hip is to have a flexible mind' (p.16). Or, for example, he thinks he is urging his mother to be more daring when he says, 'Branch out. If you can knit tea cosies you can knit skiing hats' (p. 17). Graham and his mother seem to have no friends, although the vicar calls on them – this visit resulting in one of the most amusing passages in the monologue, as Mrs Whittaker attacks the vicar's dress sense and authority. Graham has a theological point he could make about Jesus's relationship with his Mother but, as he so often records in this **tragicomedy**, he 'didn't say anything' (p. 20).

One occasion when he does say something occurs at a meeting of the 'Community Caring' circle, a passage which offers an opportunity for Alan Bennett to **satirise** a particular kind of group therapy. 'I sometimes feel a bit out of it as I've never had any particular problems' (p. 24), says Graham, with an astounding lack of self-knowledge. He takes the opportunity to discuss his anxiety about his seventy-two year old mother's romantic relationship, and the well-meaning social misfits in the group focus on the perception that he is, to use their jargon, 'defensive about sexual relationships' (p. 24). He disagrees, but again does not manage to get his point across. We guess that Graham has homosexual leanings from the references to the pornographic magazines he keeps on top of the wardrobe; he may also have had a passing interest in Joy Buckle, who taught 'Flowers in Felt and Fabric', and, if so, it would have been an interest probably scotched by his mother, who said Joy had 'some shocking eyebrows'. In any case, Graham seems to have constrained his sexual needs to what can be met by bedroom fantasies. He has pruned his emotional needs, too, to a minimum, but those needs are completely dependent on his relationship with his mother, as we realise when he goes so far as to plead with her, almost like a child: 'Don't go. Don't leave me, Mam' (p. 25).

SUSAN IN BED AMONG THE LENTILS

From her narrative we discover that Susan, the disastrous wife of a trendy, ambitious vicar, is at a loss to find her role in life. 'Once upon a time,' she says, 'I had my life planned out ... or half of it at any rate. I wasn't clear about the first part, but at the stroke of fifty I was all set to turn into a wonderful woman ... the wife to a doctor, or a vicar's wife, Chairman of the Parish Council, a pillar of the WI' (p. 33). It's the first part of her life that is causing her problems. She finds herself married to a man whose pretensions she sees through and with whom she shares neither love nor sympathy: their sexual relations are described as 'rare and desiccated conjunctions' (p. 30). She doubts the religious beliefs she is assumed to have in common with her clergyman husband and resents the demands made upon her by parish duties – which she fulfils with a striking lack of commitment or skill.

It gradually becomes clear that her unwillingness to play a part in the life of the parish is compounded by her increasing recourse to alcohol. The first hint comes when Susan mentions that the woman at the off-licence 'didn't smile', although, as she says, 'I spend enough' (p. 31). This explains perhaps why Susan had spent the Sunday afternoon avoiding Geoffrey's company, dozing and reflecting on her wasted life, 'parked in a lay-by on the Ring Road' (p. 31), when she had said she was going to deliver the parish magazine. Her accounts of embarrassing incidents which occur when she is drunk are painfully amusing. The bishop comes to lunch (an unappetising meal of 'flabby' lasagne and tinned peaches, followed by instant coffee) in order to vet her husband for promotion. It is clear he is also interested in the likely contribution of Susan, to whom he refers patronisingly as 'Mrs Vicar'. Mrs Vicar fails to respond to leading questions about the ordination of women, for example, and there is a certain **irony** in a situation where she is being questioned about a career for women whilst in the traditional role of vicar's unpaid domestic worker. Somewhat the worse for the bottle of wine, which the men did not share, she awkwardly knocks over the jug of decanted tinned milk, splashing the bishop's gaiters. The men try to cover up her clumsiness but the bishop gives her 'a funny look' and, over instant coffee, suddenly 'remembers' that he must hurry away. She obviously recognises the damage done to Geoffrey's prospects, but shows no compunction, annoying him by saying they must keep their 'fingers crossed' about his future, when he, predictably, believes they should have recourse to prayer.

In another drunken incident, Susan is on the rota for arranging flowers in the church. Depressed by the patronising parish workers, she fortifies herself with communion wine from the vestry. She does not appreciate the pretentious flower arrangement for the altar devised by one of the parishioners – 'a brown job, beech leaves, teazles, grass, that school of thought' (p. 35) – which Mrs Shrubsole calls 'Forest Murmurs'. Whilst Susan is attempting to demonstrate, with some wit, that the prickly bits could get in Geoffrey's eyes when he kneels at the altar, she topples over and hits her head. The parishioners accompany Susan home and take the opportunity to 'conduct a fact-finding survey of all the housekeeping arrangements or absence of same' (p. 36), revealing that Susan's domestic accomplishments are as inadequate as her flower displays. Having sent for the vicar, the 'fan club' proceed to make a great fuss of him and, under the guise of helpfulness, undermine further Susan's shaky position. Having slept off the effects of the communion wine, Susan goes to visit her new acquaintance and source of alcohol in Leeds, Ramesh Ramesh. They have formed the habit of talking about themselves and about religion to each other and the relationship soon has a sexual dimension. Susan's dissatisfaction with her husband and with the Anglican Church is thrown into sharp relief. The plain vicar's wife and the handsome and athletic Asian shopkeeper talk about the Hindu religion – Ramesh has a 'little statuette of a god on the wall. A god. Not The God. Not the definite article. One of several thousand, apparently ... Looks a bit more fun that Jesus, anyway. Shows me pictures of other gods, getting up to all sorts' (p. 33). Apart from the bizarre interest of making love on a bed made up on sacks of lentils, their sexual relationship is a revelation to Susan: obviously Ramesh has human understanding and sexual expertise undreamt of by Geoffrey. The opening words of Susan's narrative are: 'Geoffrey's bad enough but I'm glad I wasn't married to Jesus' (p. 30). And it is the white-clad Christ-like Ramesh – 'Like Jesus. Only not' (p. 38) – who is the key to her rejection of alcoholism. The Hindu Ramesh has all the sympathetic qualities that Susan has been unable to find in Geoffrey and Jesus, as well as a healthy enthusiasm for sex, which is enhanced rather than inhibited by his religion.

Although it is Ramesh who persuades Susan to give up alcohol, her drink problem and her apparent redemption through Alcoholics Anonymous ironically provides just the career boost that Geoffrey needs. He claims the credit for supporting her through her difficulties and in the bishop's deluded view he is 'someone with a seasoned compassion, someone who's looked life in the face' (p. 41) and the narrative draws to an end with the prospect of certain promotion for him.

For Susan, even though she is 'much smarter ... and seems a different woman' (p. 38), there is no happy ending. Unlike Alan Bennett's other *Talking Heads*, she has a good degree of self-knowledge, as well as a withering understanding of what she sees as the insincerity or even hypocrisy of her husband and his Church. She sees herself as unfulfilled and a failure, although she gets some bitter consolation, it seems, from her wilfully negative reactions to her situation.

The opening section sets the tone. There is an implication that Susan's mother was disappointed in her. Susan disrespectfully draws a parallel between her mother's self-martyring disposition and Jesus's agony in the Garden of Gethsemane. Like Jesus's disciples, who slept in his hour of need, she failed to support her mother, just as she fails to support Geoffrey or the Church. Her attitude to Church traditions is clear when she says that 'if they were really sincere about religion they'd forget flower arrangement altogether, invest in some permanent plastic jobs and put the money towards the current most popular famine' (p. 34). Equally, she does not see the communion wine as sacrosanct, but is pleased with herself when she suggests that cough mixture – 'it's red and sweet and nobody is going to notice' (p. 38) – should replace the missing wine, drunk, of course, by herself. Her narrative is interlaced with references to the New Testament and the Book of Common Prayer, and the last lines suggest she is unable completely to rid herself of her belief in the Anglican God she seems to have resented all her life.

The wit and perception which she demonstrates make the tragedy all the sadder, since it is clear that the personality which she reveals to those in the world of her parish has none of this vivacity and humour. She has encountered an approach to life which she admires in Ramesh Ramesh: he has an ethos which can encompass uninhibited sexual enjoyment, and an ability to 'take the profit and move on' (p. 41). This is something that she knows she cannot do herself. Still tied to the Anglican Church and her husband's uncongenial parishioners, she feels that her attendance at the Alcoholics Anonymous self-help meetings is just another parallel burden for her – apparently necessary, but failing to meet her real needs.

IRENE RUDDOCK IN A LADY OF LETTERS

The 'ordinary middle-aged' Miss Ruddock is a woman with a good deal of energy and we soon learn that, lacking other means of fulfilment, she takes it upon herself to report minor incidents, sometimes involving people of whom she feels suspicious, to 'the authorities'. Miss Ruddock, according to Alan Bennett's 'Introduction', 'would not accept ... that she is not a public-spirited guardian of morals', although to others she is a dangerous busybody.

Letters are her means of contact with the outside world. She is lonely. Her much-loved mother is dead and, after she died, Miss Ruddock received fifty-three letters. This comforting correspondence seems to have been the initial prompting for her endless interfering letters, using the pen her mother bought for her 'the last time she was able to go over to Harrogate. It's been a real friend' (p. 45) says Miss Ruddock – her only one, it appears. The play opens with an account of a funeral she has attended – not of a friend but of an acquaintance with whom she has spoken sometimes at the bus stop, trying to make links through the tenuous parallels in their lives. She writes to the 'director of operations' to complain of what she sees as unsatisfactory aspects of the funeral procedure and tries to extend the correspondence when he replies politely.

The scope of Miss Ruddock's letter writing is wide. She has written to the council about a broken step; to the Queen about 'dog-dirt' outside Buckingham Palace; to the press about the length of the Archbishop of Canterbury's hair; to her MP about policemen's eyesight; to sausage makers about a hair in their product. Some of her letters, for instance the one about the broken step, could be described as public-spirited, but at the other extreme her correspondence verges on the unbalanced.

As in the other plays, clues about the **narrator** are allowed to appear gradually. Miss Ruddock gets 'a bit upset' and has to take 'tablets'. Not all her letters have been so innocent, we eventually learn. An account of a visit from two police officers reveals that she has previously written malicious letters about local people which have caused great distress; she has, for instance, given 'the lollipop man a nervous breakdown' (p. 49) through her overimaginative analysis of his character. Miss Ruddock has been before the magistrates and has been bound over to keep the peace, but subsequently she has reported the young couple opposite to her doctor and others for neglecting their child. During the play she has been closely monitoring the activities of these neighbours but of course without ever making direct contact with them. Her reading of the situation is quite wrong and based on her suburban prejudices: the couple do not use a table-cloth; they need new curtains; the young man spends too long under his car; he wears a vest in the street and has a tattoo.

When Miss Ruddock tells us that the child died not of neglect but of
leukaemia, she seems strangely impassive. After this second brush with
the law, Miss Ruddock is given a suspended sentence and two social
workers to counsel her. She is contemptuous of their attempts to help and
dislikes their well-meaning familiarity. One of the social workers who
tries to empathise with her she dismisses as 'just chiming in' (p. 56). The
other offers suggestions for broadening her outlook and we learn a little
of Miss Ruddock's philosophy of life and literature. Novels she despises
for their frequently formulaic approach: when a character claims that
something has never happened before – a fire, a crash, a happy ending,
Miss Ruddock knows hat the next thing to happen will be a fire, a crash,
a happy ending. Sometimes, she tells us, she thinks that her life may be
better 'next time round' (p. 51) but then she has to admit that she does
not expect another life.

Miss Ruddock has learned nothing from her mistake over the sick
child opposite. We fear the worst when she confides that the new
community policeman 'needs reporting' for keeping too good an eye on
the housewife at number 56.

This final episode of busybodying, however, brings about an
unexpectedly fortunate **closure**. In her final scene, in prison, Miss
Ruddock – now 'Irene' to all – 'speaks very quickly and is radiant' (p. 51).
At last she has the opportunity to explore her potential and use up some
of her drive. She rapidly masters all the courses on offer and the prospect
even of a job in the real world beckons.

She is friendly and supportive to a range of women, about whose
crimes and life-styles she would have been very censorious in the past.
Now she is understanding and sympathetic, particularly to Bridget, a
prostitute who has accidentally killed her child when she was drunk.

It takes prison to break the narrow constraints of Miss Ruddock's
detached existence. 'I'm that busy' (p. 51) she says, in contrast to her
previous life of insignificant outings and interfering letter writing.
'Prison!' she says. 'This is the first taste of freedom I've had in years'
(p. 52).

The balance in this short play is tilted towards comedy rather than
tragedy. Miss Ruddock's blinkered view of life and her persistent state of
disapproval are often humorous, as are her mistakes in etiquette and her
inaccurate bad language in prison. But, like other *Talking Heads*, she is

lonely. In her case, the death of her mother – on whom she had been dependent for a lifeline to the world beyond the bay window – has left her isolated. A bay window, of course, offers a good view in several directions: in Miss Ruddock's case, it seems also to be a barrier to other than superficial understanding of what she sees. In any event, the world beyond the window has lost the comforting qualities it used to have in earlier days, when her mother knew every family in the street. She has no friend and her only relative is 'the one cousin in Canada' (p. 44). At the opening of the play, she appears never to have considered a job, so she has no work-place colleagues to relate to, either. The people whom she meets from day to day have no real interest in her and know little about her. To the doctor she is a patient whose notes suggest she can be difficult; to the vicar she is seen as a challenge to his skill in religious conversion; to the social workers she is one of many cases, perhaps hard to distinguish from each other, and dealt with in a practised, all-purpose manner which has no time to pay regard to the individual.

Given Miss Ruddock's propensity to fill her otherwise pointless life with sometimes malicious correspondence with strangers, there seems to be a tragedy in the making, and the fortunate resolution by means of a prison sentence is a dramatic twist. The narrative has led us to anticipate that Miss Ruddock will be in serious trouble with the law sooner or later, but her reaction to her imprisonment is unexpected.

It is the intimacy of prison life and the women's natural supportive interest in each other that brings Irene – no longer Miss Ruddock – into a situation where she has something to offer. Instead of her usual deeply critical view of other people, she rapidly acquires tolerance, understanding and even tact. She finds a better use for her letter writing when she helps the unattractive Shirley to formulate a letter to her imaginary boyfriend, and defends Shirley against the unkind probing of Geraldine. Her cellmate is Bridget, whose child has died, reminding us of the death of the child of the couple whom Irene had persecuted, although in this case the prostitute Bridget had killed her child in a drunken temper. Irene is able to accept this grim deed with some understanding, and perhaps there is a measure of atonement for her distressing lack of judgement in the case of her neighbours' sick child in that she is able to help Bridget through her nightmares about her child's death.

Her success in the courses run in prison and the possibility her new
qualifications offer of a life in the world outside give Irene, alone among
the *Talking Heads*, the prospect of a future to look forward to.

LESLEY IN HER BIG CHANCE

Alan Bennett writes (in the 'Introduction') that Lesley, the narrator,
'thinks that she has a great deal to offer as an actress and a person',
implying that we should understand that she hasn't. The comedy resides
in the gap between Lesley's perception of herself and her talents and our
perception of her. All of Alan Bennett's *Talking Heads* are transparent
narrators, but the characteristic is most marked in this play, which for
many will be the funniest of the six, but also perhaps the most cruel.

Lesley is a bit-part actress whose major success so far has been
as an extra in Polanski's film, *Tess*, 'the one in the back of the farm
cart wearing a shawl. The shawl was original nineteenth-century
embroidery' (p. 58) she adds, although she does not recognise the
'original nineteenth-century' novel by Thomas Hardy as the source of the
film. She attempts to add significance to her very minor role because she
imagines herself to be a 'serious' actress and likes to make considerable
play with the need to investigate the motives of the character she is
playing. She elaborates the possibilities of the one-dimensional role in the
film which offers 'her big chance' and tries to discuss it with those
involved as she believes it is necessary to help with the presentation of her
character. 'What would help your character is if you took your bikini off'
(p. 63) bluntly says an assistant on the degrading film she is making for
'export video'.

The incongruous nature of her pretensions in relation to the actual
demands of her role illustrates the nature of the humour throughout the
piece.

Lesley also prides herself on her social skills. When she meets Spud,
who is 'in films' though not at the level he suggests, she says, 'You look
an interesting person. I'm interested in interesting people. Hello' (p. 57)
demonstrating her banal party style. The transparency of her narrative
and her verbatim reports of conversations make it possible for us to
understand easily what is really going on. On this basis, we can
reinterpret much of what she says: what the other characters say, or are

reported as saying, constantly corrects Lesley's own, unperceptive version. For instance, after the audition with Simon, whom Lesley at first believes to be the director of the film, she gives herself a high score of seventy-five on the basis of a chart in a book she has been reading which gives tips on interview technique. But we know that her conversation and suggestions were so inept that Simon was expressing his astonishment about her ridiculous behaviour on the telephone to someone when she made an unannounced return visit with yet more ill-judged comments. First, as already mentioned, she shows that she does not know that the film *Tess* was based on Hardy's novel. Then she drops the director Polanski's name and says that they had a very 'open' relationship (she was an extra). This gives Simon the chance to turn to the subject of the role of Travis in the film. Travis, too, he says, is very 'open'. His sarcasm is plain when he adds that she is an 'interesting' character, who 'spends most of the film on the deck of a yacht' (p. 58). Lesley foolishly suggests that there is a link here with the small power-boat her brother-in-law keeps at Ipswich. 'Well! Snap!' says Simon (p. 58), with a heavy **irony** which we know is completely missed by the unaware Lesley. This pattern is repeated throughout the narrative.

Her pretensions and her pert, silly style mean that she is left well alone socially by most of the film crew. Even those who have been to bed with her do not reappear in her narrative. When the rest of those involved in the film are out together in the evenings, they go to the restaurant run by Lesley's stand-in for the water skiing, whom Lesley took at first to be a part-time waitress. This 'ginger' girl is the only other female mentioned and it is easy to see that her company, like that of almost any one, would be preferable to that of foolish and boring Lesley.

Lesley's vanity does not extend to what is her obviously very real physical attraction: once Gunther, the director, has seen her naked, he seems to mark her out as his prey, a situation perhaps reflected by the cat watching the trout in the animal handler's bedroom (see symbolism in Style and Language). It is, though, only on the last night that he goes to bed with her, no doubt in order to make sure that he will not have to see her again.

As well as being constantly out of her depth in understanding what is going on around her, Lesley suffers the lack of self-knowledge that afflicts most of the narrators of these plays, and does not accept that all she has to offer as an 'actress' is an attractive and photogenic body. Just as sadly, her misjudged social skills send the film team scuttling away from her – as they, too, have no use for her company and 'serious' conversation, although individually they are only too willing to take advantage of her physical charms.

The play ends at a point before the first scene (see Time and Settings). Lesley reveals that she is planning to enrich her life still further so that she will have even more to give as an actress. Nevertheless, one of her possible additional skills might be 'selling valuable oil paintings', something we know is beyond her, but which reflects her acceptance that she might need to earn a living by other means than acting.

But the first scene, which was set a week or so after the final scene of the play and the completion of the film, shows Lesley in brashly bright mood again, having worked out what she would consider a challenging remark to engage interest: 'I shot a man last week' (p. 56).

MURIEL IN SOLDIERING ON

Even though Muriel Carpenter says that she is not 'a tragic woman', her life has a considerable tragic dimension. The decline in her fortunes from the comfort of her position at the beginning of the play to friendless, pauper state at the end, has the hallmarks of a small-scale tragedy.

In the first scene she is meeting the loss of her obviously energetic and well-known husband bravely. 'Ralph touched life at many points' (p. 71) said the vicar at his funeral, and Muriel has had to entertain the many mourners who have come to pay their last respects. She describes her well-practised preparations for the late lunch with touches of humour, but with pride, too, in her capacity to 'manage' in difficult circumstances. She is confident of her organising ability.

Her shock and grief are very real and she tries to do all the 'right things', following practices that Ralph would have recommended. Advice on bereavement seems to be in short supply – the receptionist at the health centre, for instance, said that they had had some pamphlets but offered the feeble excuse that they had not bothered to reorder because children scribbled on them. However, she has no difficulty in disposing of Ralph's personal belongings: charity organisers descend upon her rapaciously with requests for his clothes, shoes, books – even his spectacles.

Of their two children, Giles and Margaret, Giles is obviously his mother's favourite. Her son seems at first to be helping his mother over her finances. Ralph, who never discussed money matters with his wife, has left her 'very nicely off', and has 'tied up a bit for Margaret' (p. 73). Muriel deceives herself throughout over Giles's character, but we soon become aware that he is helping himself to her money and that his investments on her behalf are not only unwise but disastrous. As scene follows scene, poor Muriel is reduced to cutting down on expenses, putting her sick daughter Margaret into a National Health Service Hospital, then finally selling up in order to live in a boarding-house 'flatlet' in Hunstanton. She suffers severe loneliness and poverty, which she meets with her all-purpose fortitude.

She is pleased, however, that her daughter Margaret, who has suffered with long-term problems of mental health, is now so much better that she is like a 'normal daughter' and comes to take her mother out to lunch. Unlike Giles, whose purpose, earlier in the play, in taking his mother out for a lavish meal was to make her slightly confused, Margaret has no ulterior motive. Nevertheless, Muriel has had to digest the knowledge that her daughter's illness was caused by her father's sexual abuse of his 'little girl' – knowledge which she seems able to accept with her usual stoicism. Margaret, she says, 'Doesn't seem to blame him. Wishes he were alive. Don't know what I think. Sorry for him, I suppose' (p. 78). Alan Bennett writes in his 'Introduction', 'Muriel ends up knowing her husband ruined her daughter but is no closer to realising that she had a hand in it too'. We become aware that her pride in her military-style organisation of family life and her 'soldiering on' attitude to problems disguises her lack of perception in relationships, and her failure to distinguish major from minor problems in life. It is Ralph, of course, who has been her mentor: 'It doesn't matter if you are going to get married, commit a burglary or keep a guinea pig; efficiency is the proper collation of information' (p. 72).

It seems that, although she has been a capable housewife and the competent partner of an army office and business executive, she has not really known the members of her family. She has been unaware of Ralph's preying upon his child, or of Giles's duplicitous nature. Her interest in

Margaret seems to have been just below the level of her interest in the dogs: after the funeral she does not get up at night to look after Margaret, who is disturbed, although she does get out of bed when she remembers that she has not seen to the dogs. After the financial disaster, Margaret is sent to a National Health Service institution before the dogs are disposed of.

Unlike the rest of the characters in *Talking Heads*, Muriel has been used to a comfortable middle-class life with her days passed in enjoyable activity. She has educated tastes, we gather from her interest in architecture and her hope that she might be able to go to Siena. She is used to having plenty to offer and is an experienced organiser of voluntary work and a charity money-raiser. There are many **ironies** in the development of the play: she does maintain her ability to 'soldier on', but no other aspect of her former life seems to be useful to her in her new, difficult circumstances. Previously Muriel has found a sense of community and companionship through the charities network: in the final scene we learn that she is considered only as a possible recipient of help. The fact that she strenuously declines – 'Not on your life' (p. 78) – shows not only her dismay at the clerk's mistake, but also reveals how she must view those who receive benefits or charitable help as socially unacceptable. We know that she will continue somehow on a starvation diet rather than join those who have to depend on society's support.

There is irony, too, in the fact that Margaret is actually successfully treated in the overcrowded and inconvenient National Health psychiatric hospital. The well-kept lawns and good quality cup of tea in matron's room at the private nursing home – regretted by Muriel – may well have been the pleasant façade of a regime that knew it would have been inadvisable to discover the cause of Margaret's illness – a discreet approach that would have protected Ralph but which was of no use to his daughter.

And in the end the journey Muriel makes is to Hunstanton, which is a far cry from the journey she had thought of making to the historic and architecturally beautiful Siena. Muriel's world has let her down: the financial disaster caused by Giles has revealed how little she had of lasting value in her life. Only her betrayed daughter seems to have time for her, and it is no wonder that she escapes from the unrewarding present by watching television or putting on her earphones.

DORIS IN A CREAM CRACKER UNDER THE SETTEE

In effect, we are sharing the last hours of the narrator of this play, frail, elderly Doris. She has fallen whilst doggedly dusting out of reach, strictly against the orders of her home-help, Zulema. Doris is too houseproud and a fanatical cleaner. Alan Bennett writes in his 'Introduction' that 'though she knows it's her determination to dust that has brought about her downfall, what she doesn't see is that it's the same obsession that tidied her husband into the grave'.

Even in her serious condition – her leg or hip is badly injured – she is still fussing about the gate being left open, letting in dogs and 'all sorts', and about the neighbours' leaves which have blown into her front garden. Doris's view of cleanliness and hygiene restricts her whole outlook on life. She knows that beyond her doorstep her own spotless regime does not operate – even the front garden is subject to casual urinators and neighbours' untidy leaves. In Stafford House, the old people's home that beckons, she fears that not only would she be forced to socialise but she imagines the inmates 'smelling of pee' (p. 89). There is a time dimension to her obsession – her past was different: 'people were clean and the streets were clean and it was all clean' (p.89). Like many old people she looks back regretfully to what she sees as a golden age. The present for her lacks what she values and she does not at all appreciate what the present does offer – that is, a home-help and the prospect of care in an old people's home. Zulema, the cheery sounding home-help, she sees as an adversary to be challenged and – if possible – defeated. 'She wants reporting' Doris says (p. 89) after her triumphant discovery of the half-hidden cream cracker Zulema has missed. And of course Stafford House, which Zulema describes in optimistic terms, is not to be countenanced at any price. Doris, who is quite dress conscious, gives a hilarious account of her idea of the horrors of having to mix – when it is not only the 'old lasses' but the clothes and even the teeth that are mixed up. She says, 'You go daft there, there's nowhere else for you to go but daft,' as she imagines a scene of tambourine-banging and organised chants of 'I am H.A.P.P.Y.' (p. 89).

Doris's late husband, Wilfred, whose image in their wedding photograph accompanies her throughout the play, seems to have been kept under strict control. He was allowed a small non-deciduous bush in the garden, although Doris would have preferred concrete, in spite of Wilfred's suggestion that concrete has no character. She recalls that she said, 'Never mind character, Wilfred, where does hygiene come on the agenda? With concrete you can feel easy in your mind' (p. 84). The bush represented an unusual concession, however, as all Wilfred's other plans failed to come to fruition. Doris seems to have dampened his enthusiasm for growing mushrooms in the cellar, making fretwork toys, keeping a small dog and running an allotment.

'A kiddy'd've solved all that' (p. 85), Doris says of Wilfred's half-hearted intentions to take up hobbies. It would have solved her immediate problems, too, she thinks, as she imagines her baby having lived and produced grandchildren for her: 'Wouldn't have been in this fix'. Doris's brief account of the birth of her apparently stillborn baby is central to an understanding of her character. The midwife took the baby away without letting Doris see him and wrapped him in newspaper, 'As if he was dirty' (p. 88). Doris's instincts were that 'He wasn't dirty, little thing,' showing that at that time she was able to respond to birth, one of the very messiest of events, with a normal human acceptance. The grief and disappointment seem to have marked a 'before and after' division in Doris's life. The sadness of the loss of the child is brought back to Doris in the hall, as she remembers the never-used perambulator, bought overconfidently in advance by Wilfred, and foreshadowing his subsequent failure to follow through any of his plans. Doris's crusade against dirt must have developed obsessively after the failure of their hopes of family life, which would have demanded the acceptance of a measure of mess and disorder. Now, at the end of her life, she looks back to a time when cleanliness was associated with happiness – the time before the baby's death. Not only were the streets and the people in them clean, there was a friendliness she remembers and now misses, and married life meant contentment: 'I'd wash up while he read the paper and we'd eat the toffees and listen to the wireless' (p.89).

Perhaps at the end of the play Doris does begin to accept that, in the absence of relatives or friends, society in general has been trying to look after her. She thanks the concerned policeman who has been checking up on her one more time than is necessary. But, of course, it is a crucial 'No! Thank you' for Doris, as we understand that she is stating the intention to die alone, rather than end her days in the dreaded Stafford House.

As she begins to drift in and out of consciousness, she goes back to her childhood and her earliest recollections of the association of happiness and cleanliness: 'I wish I was ready for bed. All washed and in a clean nightie and the bottle in, all sweet and crisp and clean' (p. 90).

THE UNSEEN CHARACTERS

The characters and motives of the central **narrators** have been discussed above. But beyond the narrator of each play many other characters spring to life in *Talking Heads*. The detailed accounts of events given by each narrator include, in particular, a representation of conversations that is intended to sound like **verbatim** reporting of what was said. This feature of Alan Bennett's story-telling is most effective in peopling his plays. There is also some straightforward description and comment on the narrators' attitudes to the unseen characters.

We must be aware, of course, of prejudice on the part of the narrators in what we are being told. As Alan Bennett says in his 'Introduction', we do not have an objective view of what is going on and some of the unseen characters, as well as being misunderstood (as in the case of Lesley's assessments) may also be maligned. This is an obvious implication of the single viewpoint in each **monologue**.

In *A Chip in the Sugar*, for instance, Graham in his account would like to think of his mother as a fragile and forgetful old lady, very dependent upon her son for practicalities, as well as deferring to him in the formation of her tastes and her attitudes to society. We can easily see, however, that even if physically a bit feeble – although rather livelier than Graham suggests – **Mrs Whittaker** is spirited and adaptable and still looking for adventure at seventy-two. In the interests of her own desire for what would probably be a last fling, it is clear that she is prepared to sacrifice Graham's need for stability.

Vicars do not come off well in these stories, as the dramatist acknowledges in his 'Introduction', and Mrs Whittaker trounces the clergyman who steps into her sitting-room, collecting money for famine relief. The conversation, re-enacted by Graham, is really between the **vicar** and Mrs Whittaker, with Graham very much side-lined: she has a ready line in repartee while Graham of course tells us that he 'didn't say anything'. The vicar serves the purpose of demonstrating both Mrs Whittaker's inclination to dominate and that the household's callers are formal representatives of society, rather than friends or relatives. He is deftly sketched in, though, in the account Graham gives, as trendy, earnest and superficially interested in his parishioners.

Frank Turnbull, it is easy to suspect, must have a great deal more about him than Graham allows. Their dislike of each other is partly expressed in sartorial differences – each despising the other's style of dress. Turnbull finds Graham's socks, sandals, plastic mac and flared trousers unacceptable, and Graham thinks Turnbull looks like a bookmaker in his flashy, overcolourful outfits. Turnbull is brash and reactionary, but he has a zest for life that Graham certainly lacks. Until his daughter reveals the deception, it can be seen that he has easily won the battle for the allegiance of Mrs Whittaker. As Alan Bennett writes, Graham does not realise that he is as good as married to his mother, but the story he tells is a rather grotesque version of a familiar type of domestic drama, with Mrs Whittaker the erring wife, Graham the dull husband and Frank Turnbull the dashing seducer. That the players in this eternal triangle are rather different from what might be expected adds to the comedy, of course, and disguises the pathos of the situation.

Another dimension is added to our understanding of Graham by his account of a session of 'Community Caring', involving informal group therapy. The characters of **Steve**, who runs the group, and **Leonard**, **Janice** and **Jackie**, his 'clients', are barely differentiated: they serve the purpose of reminding us of Graham's mental illness and the support that society tries to offer – a support which is not valued by Graham. He is unable to face a discussion about his mother's intended marriage in what seems to him the distasteful terminology of the group. The **parody** of social work is one of the funniest episodes in this monologue.

Susan, in *Bed Among the Lentils*, is such an engaging character that it is difficult not to take her assessment of **Geoffrey** at face value. But it does occur to us that Geoffrey, too, is having a difficult time, with a wife who questions the sincerity of the Church and her role as vicar's helpmeet. We accept that Geoffrey is ambitious, but perhaps do not see his desire for promotion within the Church as wrong in itself; it is hard not to see the dreadful lunch which Susan inflicts upon the bishop from his point of view as well – insulting food and an uncommitted wife who is also drunk.

The characters introduced to us through Susan's narration are mostly those whom she sees as part of the burden she has to bear as Geoffrey's wife. If she makes no effort for the **bishop** – sketched in as a hearty, forthright man, who, she knows, holds considerable power – she has still less to offer to parishioners. We are given glimpses of **Mr and Mrs Belcher**, who Susan suggests are puffed up with pride because both are involved in a Sunday service; **Miss Budd** and **Miss Bantock**, imagined in a fumbling lesbian encounter, as unsatisfactory as sexual relations at the vicarage; and of course the flower-arranging ladies, Mrs Belcher again, **Miss Frobisher** and the formidable **Mrs Shrubsole**. The incident involving 'Forest Murmurs', Susan's drunken fall, and the subsequent opportunities for interference by the ladies of the parish, is very entertaining and also encapsulates all that Susan finds pointless and petty about her life in the parish; the alliance of her husband with what she calls his 'fans' emphasises her isolation. What seems like something of a conspiracy between Geoffrey and his sycophantic flock could just reflect their difficulties in knowing what to do about Susan's alcoholism, although the malicious interpretation that Susan puts upon it is much more amusing.

Few characters as seen through the eyes of the narrators come over as admirable except for **Ramesh Ramesh**. The fit and handsome Hindu shopkeeper is, of course, an exotic creation, not only for his oriental religious philosophy and lack of sexual inhibitions, but also for his suggestion of an alternative way of life from that in which Susan feels herself imprisoned. He is able to 'take the profit and move on' (p. 41), something which Susan feels she should be able to do but knows she will not.

Until Irene Ruddock, in *A Lady of Letters*, finds herself in enforced contact with other women when she is sent to prison, she has no friends. She is a great letter writer and watcher of other people. Her prejudices against the **young couple** opposite are based only upon visual impressions

– no table cloth, no baby-sitter, bruised child, a tattoo; her judgement seems all the more unkind when we learn of their child's fatal illness. Like Mrs Whittaker, she routs the well-meaning **vicar** who calls upon her, startling him apparently with her claim to atheism. The **police** who call about her interfering she tries to keep at arm's length, although she avoids direct condemnation of them. She dismisses the **magistrate** who binds her over to keep the peace as 'Big fellow, navy blue suit, poppy in his button hole. Looked a bit of a drinker' (p. 50). Her two **social workers**' attempts to help are mercilessly criticised. She despises what she sees as their clumsy efforts to understand her situation and alleviate her isolation; the appearance of one of them, too – 'looks more in need of social work than I do' (p. 50) – attracts her contempt.

When the self-imposed constraint of her everyday life is changed to the real physical confinement in prison, Miss Ruddock enjoys a dramatic change in her view of her fellow-humans. The disparaging descriptions of the vicar, magistrate and social workers give way to sympathetic observation of criminals. It is not so surprising that she approves of her prison education tutors, **Mrs Proctor**, **Miss Macaulay** and **Mrs Dunlop**, but she can also describe some of her fellow-inmates with warmth and understanding. Amazingly, she is 'friends with practically everyone' (p. 51) – **Lucille**, obese, confused **Shirley**, and pretty **Bridget**, her cellmate, who has murdered her child. These characters spring to sympathetic life in Irene's narration, as what seemed likely to be a dire future for her turns into an unexpectedly positive conclusion.

In *Her Big Chance* we are in the seedy world of third-rate film-making. 'Actress' could be only a courtesy title for Lesley, whose experience has previously been limited to playing film extras or walk-on television parts. Her function as 'Travis' in a cheap sex and violence film we soon see is to provide nude scenes. She is unable to cope with the few lines the script offers her, although she does not realise this. We feel almost sorry for the harassed film crew who have to deal with her pretensions and lack of acting ability. Lesley 'collects' people, we learn at the beginning of the **monologue**, and she presents her collection – the film crew – to us one by one: **Spud**, the electrician; **Simon**, the general assistant; **Scott**, in charge of wardrobe and make-up; **Nigel**, the director's assistant; **Terry**, a cameraman; **Kenny**, the animal handler; and **Gunther**, the director.

Those who want to are able to get into bed with her; the cynical preliminaries are naïvely related to us by Lesley, who obviously thinks that she is recording vivacious, interesting conversations that she has had with the predatory Spud, Terry, Kenny and Gunther. Predictably, none of them pursues her acquaintance.

The characters who are not interested in her physical charms are sometimes verbally quite scathing, although Lesley is not perceptive enough to spot this. Simon is sarcastic, although she does not see it; but he lets her down lightly when he gets rid of her at the end of the audition, saying of her extravagant suggestions about Travis, 'I'm most grateful. You've given me a lot of ideas' (p. 60), but we understand only too well that his politeness covers a relief that she is going. Scott, the embittered wardrobe man, is very cutting – even Lesley realises this – but she puts this down to his personal problems and is thus able to ignore what he says. Nigel, the director's assistant, is apparently used to handling actresses' inflated ideas of their talents; however, we can see from Lesley's reported conversations during filming that she is driving him to breaking point, when she thinks she is being constructive. Eventually, he is unable to maintain a reasonable civility and says coarsely, 'Who do you think you're playing, Emily Brontë? Gunther wants to see your knockers' (p. 64).

Lesley tells us at the beginning of *Her Big Chance* that her professionalism requires her to be involved in her work; she seems to think that she is giving an intelligent account of the way in which she has forged relationships with the members of the team, and has contributed to the development of the director's vision. Since her account is perceived to be entirely illusionary, the secondary characters in this play greatly influence our coming to a more realistic understanding of the story.

At the opening of *Soldiering On* Muriel Carpenter, surrounded by friends and acquaintances, seems to view them mainly in terms of management or organisation: the mourners at Ralph's funeral have to be introduced to each other and fed afterwards. Muriel is in charge, but she is appreciative of those she sees as assistant organisers – **Mabel**, her housekeeper, who has produced a soup that sounds rather dull, and family, who help out with guided tours and polite conversation. Muriel, in spite of her grief, maintains her skill as an accomplished hostess and introduces people to each other without necessarily knowing them herself. She and Mabel in a brief interlude have 'a good laugh and a good cry' before 'hurling themselves back into the fray' (p. 71). It is all rather like an army exercise. And so is the way in which Muriel is always prepared to move on in response to circumstances. It is clear that Mabel has been with her for a long time – she has had to polish the furniture 'all these years' and is familiar with Margaret's precarious state of health. But after the crash Muriel, although perhaps suggesting that Mabel may now be looking for a husband, moves on – as though to another 'posting' – with no backwards look or further comment on Mabel.

Of Muriel's fellow workers for charity who descend on the house like locusts in the battle for charity shop items from amongst Ralph's belongings, only **Angela** stands out. The first reference to her is of 'awful Angela Gillespie'; she advises Muriel about the disposal of the 'jumble', buys a long fancied corner cupboard at the auction, and says what every one but Muriel has long known about crooked Giles. But 'awful Angela' remains the only person from the 'old days' still in touch with Muriel at the end of the story. We cannot tell whether this is a further trial for Muriel or whether she now sees Angela in a different light. In rather the same way, the young psychiatrist of whom Muriel disapproves is able to help **Margaret** towards a cure. Also, it is her undervalued daughter who is in touch with her mother by the end of the narrative, and not her dreadful favourite, **Giles**.

Giles is one of the few real villains to appear in *Talking Heads* and the tension in this play is heightened by his mother's failure to realise how little he cares for her and how cruelly she is being exploited. The smug safety of his own life contrasts painfully at the end with Muriel's impoverishment, and his pretended distress at her position results in what must be the final blow – the loss of contact with her grandchildren. Margaret, on the contrary, moves from the kind of sub-human status Muriel affords her at the beginning of the narrative into a warm, human dimension. **Ralph** remains something of a mystery; much loved and yet little known by his wife; a figure widely respected in the world and a betrayer of his family at home – perhaps we recognise him as one of those bafflingly kindly wrongdoers who figure in the crime pages of the press.

The unseen characters in this monologue spring to life as they do in the other plays, although there is less verbatim re-enacting of conversations – it would not be Muriel's style. We get more reported speech and straightforward narrative. Alan Bennett shows the same skill, however, in using these characters to reveal much of what we know about the central narrator. In this particular play, there is a sense of a background thronged with the people who surround Muriel in the first scenes, which contrasts with her wretchedly solitary state at the end.

Wilfred and Zulema, even though invisible, play the supporting roles in *A Cream Cracker Under the Settee*. Another of Alan Bennett's lonely characters, without friends or relatives, Doris spends much of her time in the play in remembering her husband, **Wilfred**, and their earlier married days. Wilfred comes over as good-natured and even dominant in the first stage of their marriage – he insists on buying the bargain perambulator before the baby is born We realise, however, that at some stage in their life after the disappointment about the baby Wilfred's spirit has been broken. He does not carry through any of his plans and Doris never for a moment imagines that her interest in hygiene and cleanliness could have been soul destroying for Wilfred.

Even in what we know will be her final hours she shows a keen interest in Zulema's cleaning, or lack of it. If thoughts of Wilfred provide Doris's only link with a world that she once found kindly, **Zulema** represents the world 'outside' from which Doris now shrinks.

Zulema represents the forces of society at large, which have taken on responsibility for Doris, very much against her will. 'Outside' are the neighbours, unknown and often changing; dirty little boys; tiresome religious cranks. With them she includes the dreaded Stafford House, the old people's home which inevitably lies in wait; perhaps the policeman who keeps an eye on her; and certainly Zulema, in Doris's eyes the agent of the social services. Looking past Doris's prejudiced description of Zulema, we can see a well-intentioned home-help, who offers sensible advice to Doris and probably cleans up well enough. She is friendly and cheerful and tries to make Doris see that Stafford House is not the awful place she believes it to be. We can also tell, of course, that Doris is only one of many elderly or infirm people that Zulema must visit in the course of a week, and that her interest in Doris would have to be described as professional.

Unlike some of the other short plays, *A Cream Cracker Under the Settee* is thinly populated, but – as in the other **monologues** – the unseen characters play crucial roles in our understanding of the narrator. Here Wilfred and Zulema may seem very different figures in Doris's household, and yet each of them she sees as an enemy in her endless battle against dust and dirt.

Monologue as tragicomedy

The literary term for each of these plays is **monologue** or **monodrama**. The terms refer to a single person speaking alone. Most prayers, lyric poems and poetic laments are monologues, as are **soliloquies** – usually self-examination or self-revelation, as in, for example, *Hamlet* (1601) or *Othello* (1604). A monodrama is a monologue in the form of a play in which there is only one character, for example *Krapp's Last Tape* (1958), by Samuel Beckett (1906–89).

Each of the above definitions can be seen as relevant to a study of *Talking Heads*; for instance, we recognise the lament that lies beneath the narrator's story, as we recognise the self-revelation if not the self-examination of the Shakespearean soliloquy. Perhaps because in a literary sense we are trained to accept the monologue, the strangeness of our relationship to the narrator is not at first apparent. In the first place, whom is the narrator addressing? In *Soldiering On* Muriel Carpenter at the end says, 'I wouldn't want you to think this was a tragic story', making 'you' or us the identified confidantes of her story. Otherwise, a viewer/listener/reader is rarely acknowledged. Indeed, the whole problem for these mostly lonely or isolated people is that they have no one in whom to confide. This puts the viewer into the position of a *voyeur*, or an eavesdropper. Although in no cases do the narrators examine their own responsibilities for their unsatisfactory position in the world, nevertheless their **transparency** in revealing themselves unwittingly to the viewer suggests an invasion of privacy. This leaves the viewer – who is probably helpless with laughter, for the plays are very funny – nevertheless feeling uneasy. With the exception perhaps of Susan, the very self-aware vicar's wife, the characters' intended purpose is not to provoke laughter but somehow to justify themselves, to call attention to their plight. Alan Bennett manipulates our response, first by making us laugh and then by making us accept that, in the end, the lives of these characters are no laughing matter – unless we take the view that in any case life is something of a comical charade and that we, too, inevitably show symptoms of what is after all probably only the natural human condition.

An aspect of the monologue which is well worth bearing in mind is that it has often been used to serve the purposes of comedy, Music hall turns, particularly in the first half of the twentieth century, included monologues or recitations which could be seriously intended but which, much more often, were humorous. A favourite was the Northern comic **epic**, *Albert and the Lion*, performed by Stanley Holloway (1890–1982). Later in the century artistes such as Mabel Constanduros (d.1957 'aged 77') and Joyce Grenfell (1919–79) developed music hall turns which were much more subtle. Joyce Grenfell's one-woman show could be seen as anticipating *Talking Heads* in that her characters invariably had the 'artlessness' which Alan Bennett describes as being a major attribute of his **narrators**. This resulted in a **dramatic irony** which meant that her audience apparently understood more of what was happening on stage than did the person she was portraying, who might be a relentlessly cheery kindergarten teacher, for instance, or a self-absorbed music lover. Her characters were not touched by tragedy, however, other than that of a failure in self-knowledge, and there was a comfortable collusion between the author – who resumed her own personality at the end of each monologue – and the audience over what was going on.

Monologues such as those of Joyce Grenfell had central characters who were middle-class, often mildly pretentious, and the resulting humour was gentle. Other comedians provided more robust fare, and a music hall comedian such as Norman Evans (d. 1962 'aged 61') often played a Northern housewife, who could be seen as a rough and ready forerunner of a Mrs Whittaker or Doris. This favourite character, an elderly woman with unstable teeth and bosom, who always appeared as though with her elbows resting on a back-garden wall, was very crudely sketched and much of the comedy relied upon *double entendre*. However, 'her' incongruous juxtaposition of ideas and re-enacting of sharp conversations find at least an echo in Alan Bennett's short plays.

In *A Chip in the Sugar*, for example, Graham's mother is the source of many a snappy conversation that would make material for a stand-up comedian (an entertainer who relies for comic effect on his particular way of delivering jokes and anecdotes). Graham reports an exchange she has had with the vicar, when she asks where he got his shoes. He says:

> 'They're training shoes.' She said, 'Training for what? Are you not fully qualified?' He said, 'If Jesus were alive today, Mrs Whittaker, I think you'd find these would be the type of shoes he would be wearing.' 'Not if his mother had anything to do with it,' she said. 'She'd have him down Stead and Simpson's and get him some good brogues.' (p. 21)

A vicar is at the receiving end again in *A Lady of Letters*, when Miss Ruddock challenges his proffered cross as a means of identification, since – as she says – even hooligans now wear them, probably in their ears. Doris, in *A Cream Cracker Under the Settee*, rehearses a pert conversation with Zulema after she finds the cracker that Zulema has failed to notice in her rather sketchy cleaning. Wilfred, too, has been the recipient in the past of some telling remarks about the nature of concrete and hygiene.

All three of these doughty ladies share a combative style and a turn of phrase that many a music hall entertainer would recognise as guaranteeing comic success. This knockabout stuff, however, is only one of the weapons in Alan Bennett's writer's armoury: his comedy arises from many sources. In *Bed Among the Lentils* Susan, the vicar's wife, is a witty woman and unlike the other narrators in that she is very self-aware, even though this does not prevent her from being trapped in an unhappy situation from which she unable to escape. The sense of unease that creeps into what can seem like an intrusion into privacy in relation to some of the characters does not operate here, and Susan's subversive questioning and cynical assessments of others' motives are purely enjoyable. We can relish the theological posers she presents to her self-seeking husband – by suggesting that cough mixture will serve perfectly well as an emergency substitute for communion wine, for instance, or by asking him if he thinks Jesus ever 'smirked'. She tells the tale of the flower arranging with a pointed wit, as amused by her own dire role in the incident as by the account of the pretensions of Mrs Shrubsole's 'Forest

Murmurs', and the sycophancy of what she calls her husband's 'fan club'. Amusing, too, is her recording of her sexual encounters with Ramesh Ramesh by marking the occasions with reference to parallel events in the Church calendar: a particularly satisfactory meeting, for example, she mentions as having taken place amongst the lentils on the second Sunday after Trinity, and yet another on the feast of St Simon and St Jude. She is, it seems, enjoying a private, idiosyncratic revenge upon Geoffrey and the Church.

Muriel, the practised hostess of *Soldiering On*, is not sharply witty, like Susan, but she has a light, almost flippant, style which is the verbal manifestation of her stoicism. She gives, for instance, a wryly humorous account of the charity scavengers who descend upon her in search of loot in the form of her late husband's clothes, books, shoes, and so on. Later, a similar group of people arrives at the auction of her house and contents, keen once again to benefit from her misfortunes; she assesses their motives shrewdly, but amusingly. Muriel's recognition that her organising skills are no longer in demand is told, too, with humour – bitter, this time – when she offers her services to the community in the small town to which she has moved, only for it to be assumed that she is asking for assistance. As she says, 'message received and understood. The old girl's past it' (p. 78).

Her Big Chance is a very funny play in which the ridiculous narrator completely fails to understand what is going on in the events which she describes. Poor Lesley thinks that she is a perceptive actress and a well-developed individual. Her naïve re-enacting of the many conversations she has during her audition and brief filming experience show that in each case she is judged and found wanting. Ignorant, pretentious, incompetent – her inadequacies are brutally revealed through her comic misjudgements of the success of her social and professional encounters. The humour in this play is destructive, however, since it withholds our sympathy from the narrator in a way that is not evident in the other *Talking Heads*.

Comedy of one sort or another, then, is very much to the fore in these plays, but each has a tragic dimension as well. Tragedy is not perhaps a word readily associated with the situations of the narrators in *Talking Heads*. In dramatic terms, it belongs traditionally to heroic plays about the downfall of the great: Oedipus and Agamemnon are classic figures of Greek tragedy; Othello and King Lear are examples of Shakespeare's great tragic figures. Graham, Susan, Irene, Lesley, Muriel, Doris ... do they belong in that company? They are little people. Yet modern classics have brought an acceptance that ordinary people can be the subjects of tragic drama, following great nineteenth-century dramatists such as Ibsen (1828–1906) or Chekhov (1860–1904), whose **tragicomedies** create the same kind of emotional confusion as that of which Alan Bennett is a contemporary master. Some examples of tragicomedies of everyday life from this century could include some of the plays of Tennessee Williams (1911–83), who produced searing images of tragic provincial life; *Mother Courage*, by Bertholt Brecht (1898–1956); the absurdist works of Samuel Beckett (1906–89) and Tom Stoppard's (b. 1940) *Rosencrantz and Guildenstern Are Dead* (1966). *Death of a Salesman* (1949), by Arthur Miller (b. 1915) is a particularly memorable example of the tragedy of a 'little' man. Willy Loman, his defeated salesman, in fact demands the same kind of attention from the audience as do Alan Bennett's narrators: 'Attention, attention must be finally paid to such a person,' insists his wife. The narrators of *Talking Heads* require the same of us.

TIME AND SETTINGS

Alan Bennett's approach to settings and chronology rings the changes, within the obvious constraints of the form, to suit each **narrator**'s story. The time scale, for instance, varies from one short day in *A Cream Cracker Under the Settee* to a considerable length of time, perhaps a year or more, in *Bed Among the Lentils* or *Soldiering On*. Equally, in so far as the settings are concerned, he limits the telling of the narrative in *A Chip in the Sugar* to Graham's bedroom, whereas in *Her Big Chance* there is a widening out from the opening setting of Lesley's flat to scenes where she is between work sessions on the film.

Graham's room in a house in northern England is spartan, a single man's room, and this is the background to his story throughout *A Chip in the Sugar*. The humour, as usual, is balanced by the bleakness of the narrator's situation, and we find ourselves forced into a quite painful degree of intimacy with his problems. This tension is created not least by the claustrophobic setting. His room is Graham's refuge, evidently, a place where he can be safe, but it becomes clear during the play that he feels besieged there, too, as he wonders if the house is being watched.

The play proceeds chronologically, like an occasional diary. There are five scenes, the first a long account of Mrs Whittaker's meeting with her admirer from the distant past. The other scenes, over an unidentified time scale of probably a few weeks, reveal the development of the romance and its ending when Frank's deception is uncovered. Two of these scenes are described as being at night: the fourth scene, in which Graham is sitting in his pyjamas on his unmade bed, marks his point of deepest despair, and the night setting and his inability to sleep add to this mood. The final scene is also at night, but Graham – his confidence returned – has been reading one of his magazines before he sits comfortably in his chair. His life has resumed its even tenor and, for the time being, all is well again: no imaginary person has been watching the house, but a real person has delivered him from his predicament; the symptoms of his illness have not returned; his mother is restored to him.

In *Bed Among the Lentils* Alan Bennett goes rather further afield in his settings, and the time span of the narrative is considerable. There are scenes in the country church near Leeds – in the vestry and in the side chapel; in the vicarage there are two scenes in the kitchen and the final one in the drawing room. The church scenes support central incidents in the **monologue**. In the side chapel Susan is polishing a candlestick – a reference to her duties in the church and perhaps to the later flower arranging debacle. The vestry, the cupboard door now locked, was one of Susan's sources of alcohol, in the form of the communion wine. Alan Bennett uses the vicarage scenes to show Susan's reformation (probably temporary), as the careless drunkard of the kitchen becomes the perfectly presentable smart woman of the drawing room.

The clues to the time span of this monologue show that the five scenes take place over quite a period of time, probably about a year. Appropriately, the dramatist charts the events by means of dates in the Church calendar. Susan's first scene takes place before Easter; the fourth scene dates a sensually memorable visit to Ramesh as taking place on the second Sunday after Trinity (June) and the fifth refers to another visit to Ramesh on the Feast of St Simon and St Jude (28 October), although since that time Susan has undergone probably quite lengthy treatment for alcoholism and 'seems a different woman'. The use of dates from the Church calendar marks time conveniently and it also makes an ironic comment, considering the nature of Susan's activities.

There is a marked dramatic twist at the end of *A Lady of Letters* and the sets support the plot. Most of the play's seven scenes take place in Miss Ruddock's sitting room in a town in northern England, as she pursues her self-appointed duty of observing her neighbours through the bay window; the room is her centre of operations, and Alan Bennett creates the impression in the first four scenes that, when she is not on the look-out, she is busy at her letter writing. The following scene, forwarding the plot, is set at the police station, or perhaps the social services office. Miss Ruddock is in her outdoor clothes and has had what we learn is a second brush with the law. In the sixth scene – the last but one – Miss Ruddock is back home, but we suspect that her suspended sentence will come into force when she becomes overcurious about the new policeman's pattern of calls.

Sure enough, in the last scene Miss Ruddock, now 'Irene' to all, is in prison, although to our surprise she is revelling in the opportunities prison life offers her. Her change from conventional clothes to a tracksuit underlines what has happened. The settings have helped to support the narrative: in particular, Miss Ruddock's displacement from her room to the police station in the fifth scene prepares us to some extent for her sudden imprisonment in the final one. In some scenes time of day is not mentioned, otherwise it is daytime, except for the sombre fourth scene, set at dusk, which precedes her arrest and in which Miss Ruddock explains her feeling that the street nowadays is full of strangers who do not keep an eye on the neighbourhood.

The time scale seems to be linked to the unknown sick child who lives opposite Miss Ruddock. The first scene refers to the young family having just moved in; subsequent scenes show Miss Ruddock's developing disquiet about them; we are told about the death of the child in the fifth scene; finally, in the seventh scene, references to Irene's cellmate Bridget's dead child offer an echo of the neighbours' tragedy.

The time scale linking the dead children matters: Irene is a changed character in the final scene and her understanding attitude to Bridget's guilt and horror about her dead child serves as an illustration of her redemption.

The first two and the last scenes in *Her Big Chance* are set in Lesley's flat in Bromley and act as a frame, representing her normal, everyday life. In the third and fourth scenes, the opportunity is taken to show Lesley waiting to work on the film she sees as an opportunity to impress with her imaginary acting skills. The small, dismal dressing-room and the anonymous hotel room specified are as comments on the reality of the shoddy film with which Lesley is involved.

The time scale in this play breaks with the straightforward chronology established in the other *Talking Heads*. Alan Bennett has chosen to begin his narrator's account about a week after the end of filming. Then, in a series of **flashback** scenes, we follow the sequence of events over what seems to be a rather hurried film-making at Lee-on-Solent until Lesley is back home again. The final scene is set at dusk and Lesley is perhaps a little bit more thoughtful than usual. Although she seems to believe that she will 'have to live' with the fame that Gunther has **ironically** told her is coming her way, she is also recognising that she needs to acquire 'another skill', perhaps subconsciously understanding that her acting future may be limited. In contrast, the first scene of the play – which takes place last of all, chronologically – is set in the morning, and Lesley is at her most horribly vivacious. Her unjustified optimism has returned; she has digested her film experience and turned it into what she no doubt considers a riveting story that she will tell to anyone she can persuade to listen.

The sets go quite a long way towards telling the story in *Soldiering On*. By the fourth scene, Muriel's once 'comfortable home' has become bare, stripped by the auctioneers; in the last scene she is discovered in a 'plain boarding-house room', where her penurious state has forced her to take up residence. This sequence reinforces our understanding – from the second scene onwards – that Giles is likely to cause her financial downfall. Setting the last scene in the evening helps to establish the mood for Muriel's acceptance that her previous life is over, and that the evening of her days is to be unfulfilled and lonely.

This **monologue** begins somewhere in East Anglia in April and ends 'out of season' in Hunstanton. As in *Bed Among the Lentils*, for this play to be credible quite a lengthy time span is needed – probably a year or more. The dramatic urgency of the story, however, has to be maintained, so that the passage of time within the play is not emphasised and events seem to follow in fairly rapid succession.

The final play, like the first, has a somewhat claustrophobic atmosphere, underlined by the fact that the setting of all four scenes is Doris's home – to her a hygienic fortress against the dirt and confusion of the world. In the first three scenes Doris is hoping to attract attention and help from 'outside' after her accident. By the fourth scene she has realised that help from outside will lead to the old people's home she dreads; she takes the decision that she will let nature takes its course and die in her own home. The change of settings supports this sequence of Doris's thought in the play: by the third scene, still thinking of rescue, she has reached the front door – the nearest point to people and the life 'outside' which she mistrusts. Her withdrawal to the sitting room reflects her defiant, or wilful rejection of the life that society offers her.

In *A Cream Cracker Under the Settee* the action gives the impression of being virtually continuous, although some hours must pass from her fall after Zulema's visit in the morning until the darkness that signals approaching night and, of course, Doris's death.

We do not see what would have been Doris's painful and undignified progress across the floor between scenes. Doris does not move far and, though they are not immobilised, neither do the rest of the *Talking Heads;* their fixed positions help to give these **narrators** something of their mesmerising quality.

This commentary about Alan Bennett's use of time and settings obviously refers directly to screened productions of the plays. Even if these monologues are being read as short stories, however, it is relevant to consider these matters. To read the stage directions about settings will help to widen the scope of the imagination, and it is as natural when reading a short story as when watching a play to be aware of its time scale.

In these short plays the themes are usually those long associated with the human condition: loneliness and alienation, a failure to understand others, a lack of self-knowledge.

Alan Bennett's characters are very much those of the end of the century: the predicaments in which they find themselves mean that they are individuals at odds with contemporary society, the traditional structures of which – the Church, the family, community – have changed, yet somehow these characters have found means of surviving.

LONELINESS AND ALIENATION FROM A CHANGED SOCIETY

All the characters in these monologues are lonely or they are threatened with loneliness, and this loneliness stems from misreading the rules of a changed society.

Miss Ruddock, for instance, is lost in a society that no longer has any firm boundaries. In the past a neighbourly interest was welcomed, but no personal contact has ever been initiated by her with the young family she is spying upon, nor by them with her. The Church, which once offered order and security, is debased: when the vicar offers to prove his identity by showing her his cross, she dismisses the gesture by saying that a cross does not mean anything nowadays and anyone can wear it. It is no longer a potent symbol. Only in prison does she find a satisfactory structure to life.

Muriel Carpenter faces loneliness through a breakdown in family values, first by gradually facing the realisation that her husband has sexually abused their daughter, and secondly by the betrayal by the son, who should be protecting rather than stealing from her.

Doris, entirely alone, looks back nostalgically to an ordered past when streets were clean and neighbours were friendly, and strangers did not urinate in your garden. The only alternative to her loneliness which is on offer is institutionalisation.

Most of the plays make the audience conscious of the efforts of the various organisations of the welfare state to cope with the needs of the narrators and the unseen characters. These efforts are seen as poor substitutes for support for the individual traditionally given by family, friends and neighbours, and are grudgingly or ungratefully received by the beneficiaries, as are the well-intentioned visits of the clergy.

ILLNESS

Several characters suffer from mental illness: Graham, Miss Ruddock and Muriel Carpenter's daughter all have to take 'tablets'. This can, of course, represent medical progress or can seem in *Talking Heads* to show the National Health Service's universal response to individual problems. Something like a cure, however, is achieved for Margaret Carpenter (**ironically**, not in the comfortable private sector), and Graham is not negative about his doctor, Dr Chaudhury – although he uses the prescription of 'a stable environment' as emotional blackmail to try to stop his mother from remarrying. Miss Ruddock is someone who never doubts her own judgement, and she attacks the unfamiliar doctor and the manufacturers of her 'tablets' when she calls at the surgery. In the end, she flushes away her prescription down the lavatory. She accepts that she 'gets a bit upset' but clearly thinks that it is not medication she needs but support in her role as guardian of public morality. In the cases of both Graham and Miss Ruddock, when they have what they want from life they are not ill: Graham apparently manages well when he is assured of his mother's company; Miss Ruddock positively blooms when she is forcibly integrated into prison society.

Margaret Carpenter's case is different: her illness is caused by her father's abuse and when her father dies we assume that the secrecy and silence that have been the result of the betrayal can be broken. Her illness is not the rather vague malaise that affects Graham and Miss Ruddock, and which may be seen in *Talking Heads* as a **metaphor** for dissatisfaction with their lives.

UNHAPPINESS

The **narrators** find different ways in which to be unhappy. Graham's loneliness is assuaged only by the company of his mother and his pride maintained by his dominance of her thoughts and tastes. The world outside is too difficult for him, it seems, and his taste in pornography suggests, too, that he might have difficulty in coming to terms with his sexuality. Nevertheless, whilst he is secure at home and can keep alive his mother's interest in him, he survives and enjoys sharing his views on current affairs and his outings with Mrs Whittaker.

We wonder if tragedy looms, however; Mrs Whittaker is old and frail and disappointed – soon he will be alone.

Susan's unhappiness is harder to analyse. The dramatist has created a witty, complex narrator who is not so helpless that she could not have avoided a loveless marriage and a role which ties her to the Church in which she has lost faith. Her disappointment seems to relate to her whole world and drink is her means of escape. When she finds herself, almost by accident, in an exotic affair, we see that she needs a lover rather than a husband shared by all the parish. For a while she finds Ramesh's unfamiliar philosophy refreshing, but he is able to 'move on' and she is not. She survives by mocking not only what she sees as the pointless activities of her life but herself as well. She 'seems a different woman' in the last scene, but we probably have little confidence in any future happiness. Alan Bennett's narrator is a subversive character, not one of society's more comfortable members.

Miss Ruddock's story does have a happy ending. When she is brought face to face with some of life's more brutal realities in prison, she is able to exchange her extreme isolation for participation in the excitement of learning and the fascination of being part of the prison community – and actually being able to offer sympathy and help. At the beginning of her **monologue**, she feels painfully (like Doris in *A Cream Cracker Under the Settee*) that neighbours are not what they used to be, that there are too many changes in her street and that the world beyond her front door is unknown and dangerous. It is very much worse for some people, she discovers in prison, than she could ever have imagined. Alan Bennett uses this discovery as her means of redemption.

LACK OF SELF-KNOWLEDGE

Muriel Carpenter says that she is 'not a tragic woman' (p. 79), and Miss Ruddock would not accept the magistrate's comment that she was 'more to be pitied than anything else' (p. 50). It is perhaps part of their strategies for survival that the narrators do not see themselves as pitiable and if Alan Bennett's central theme is that the human condition is **tragicomic,** then their lack of self-knowledge contributes to both the tragedy and the comedy of the narrators. It also reminds us uncomfortably of the French poet Baudelaire's (1821–67) famous indictment of his reader: '*Hypocrite lecteur! Mon semblable, mon frere!*' (Hypocritical reader, my double, my brother!). These narrators live in a world which we share, and which we understand only too well.

Poor Lesley in *Her Big Chance* lacks self-knowledge to a degree beyond redemption. Alan Bennett's theme of loneliness is present here, too, and all the more poignant for Lesley's failure to recognise what a lonely woman she is. Resolutely bright and cheerful, apparently dedicated to self-improvement and professionalism, she seems to believe that she is a success socially and as an actress. In reality, she is hardly able to communicate on a human level – except in bed, perhaps. Alan Bennett shows her personality to be an artificial product of her belief that there are rules to be learned about human behaviour and that they can be found in pseudo-scientific handbooks. In failing to respond naturally to other people but trying to manipulate them to her advantage – as advised by her superficial reading – she in fact becomes easy prey to the manipulations of others. Alan Bennett has dealt savagely with this **narrator**, perhaps as revenge for his past suffering at auditions with actors and actresses, of whom he says he has 'met dozens' like Lesley.

Muriel Carpenter is another character who not only lacks self-awareness but is sometimes seriously unable to understand what is going on. She prides herself on surviving – 'soldiering on' – and at the end of the monologue challenges loneliness with her radio and television. She also challenges our view of her as a tragic woman, though there is more of tragedy than comedy in her decline, particularly since Alan Bennett lets us know that her own rose-spectacled view of her dreadful son is the cause of it.

THE 'LITTLE' PERSON IN SOCIETY

If the main themes of Alan Bennett's *Talking Heads* are loneliness and failure to understand life and oneself, he also pays respect to the right to attention of the 'little' person in society. Foolish, wilful, vain, mistaken, not quite truthful, as they might be, the narrators are given substance and demand a hearing. Their problems may be the problems of ordinary and often unfortunate people at a particular point in time, but there is a universality about their narratives that touches us and finds us confused between tears and laughter.

If you have ever made a recording of a discussion or of what seemed like a lively conversation, you will know how – once out of context – the dialogue sounds incomplete, fragmented and much less interesting than you would have expected.

It is easy to recognise therefore that, whilst persuading us that we are listening to a monologue employing everyday speech, Alan Bennett nevertheless has had to bring much writer's skill to bear on his raw material. He obviously has a very good ear for the nuances of speech and many of the memorable phrases of his monologues probably owe their inclusion to a writer's notebook record of snatches of overheard conversation. There are many **loose sentences** and the language is informal, **colloquial** and makes use of some **dialect**, since his task has been to create convincingly naturalistic speech, which carries the whole burden of character realisation and the telling of a story. In fact, each narrator tells two stories – an account of events as the speaker sees things, and the story that we are meant to understand through our own assessment of what has really been going on. In each of the plays, Alan Bennett makes us gradually realise that these are **unreliable narrators** – that we are meant to see beyond what they are saying and to understand the real story, 'to the meaning of which they are not entirely privy', as he writes in the 'Introduction'. In this way a collusion is invited between the dramatist and the viewer or reader, and the means by which this is done demands skills far beyond what has been called 'gossip into drama'.

These general comments apply to all the *Talking Heads* monologues and it is this approach – the apparently realistic speech and the **transparency** of the narrator – which links them stylistically. Each narrator is, however, memorably distinct, as is the story told. (The Textual Analyses offer detailed consideration of the style and language of passages from three of the monologues.)

Graham's is one of Alan Bennett's 'northern' voices. His view of life is a gloomy one, and this is highlighted by contrast with the merrriment of his mother and Frank Turnbull. A repeated phrase by which we remember Graham is 'I didn't say anything' – expressing both his disapproval and also his inability to influence events. Graham is fussy, and very interested in domestic details, and his gloom and his fussiness come together in the title of the monologue, *A Chip in the Sugar*. This distasteful detail in the 'common' red café where Frank takes them can also be seen as a metaphor for vulgar Frank's interruption of what Graham sees as his pleasant existence with his mother.

The title of *Bed Among the Lentils*, too, is a literal description as well as carrying the suggestion that Susan needed an exotic escape from her predictable husband and his unpleasing embraces. Her narrative is interlaced with quotations from the Anglican ritual in which her life is steeped. Susan is full of questions which she does not always voice: she would like to ask Geoffrey whether he actually believes in God or whether he just does a job like any other. She also questions her own failure to find fulfilment in life, where Alan Bennett uses something approaching stream of consciousness passages, an elaboration of his technique which he uses very little in *Talking Heads*, because the narrator's first purpose is to unfold a fairly brisk plot.

Susan's monologue – again, unusually in *Talking Heads* – is full of ironic comments: for instance, when Geoffrey preaches a sermon concluding that the money put in the offertory plate is a symbol of offering to God everything in life including sex, Susan comments, 'I could only find 10p'. Susan is perfectly aware of the irony in this remark, and we share the humour with the character in this particular monologue, rather than – as in the others – with the dramatist. (See Text 1 of Textual Analysis for further detailed commentary on a passage from this monologue.)

With Miss Ruddock in the sarcastically named *A Lady of Letters*, we are back with what might seem a particularly northern relish for the supposedly correct approach to the minutiae of everyday life. She is aggressive and has a scathing word or two for nearly everyone and everything. Her narrative is brisk and she has a strident confidence in her knowledge of etiquette which makes her one or two solecisms more amusing. For instance, she congratulates herself on taking up smoking, since she believes it will be useful if she ever has to toast the Queen. Alan Bennett seems to imbue her fountain pen, the 'trusty Platignum', with a symbolic quality. It is the cause of both her downfall and her prospect of a new life, and to Miss Ruddock, it is a reminder of her mother, who bought it for her on one of her last outings before she died. Her mother and the memories of a happier past – an imagined golden age – are linked with the pen. Although the pen is implicated in the slanderous letters written by Miss Ruddock, it is included in her redemption, since in prison she puts her letter writing skills to a more sympathetic use. (See Text 2 in Textual Analysis for detailed commentary on a passage from this monologue.)

The would-be sophisticated Lesley in *Her Big Chance* – an **ironic** title – is presented as unrelentingly pretentious and tedious. Alan Bennett swamps her speech with clichés, something that he limits in the other monologues, where the **narrators** – although speaking **colloquially** – are given individual patterns of speech, and clichés are not the most important means of establishing character. Lesley's first two brief paragraphs, however, show the dependence of her monologue on cliché: 'look to the future'; 'under your belt'; 'line of duty'; takes in their stride'; 'tussle with my conscience'; 'things were never going to be the same again'; 'a woman at the crossroads' all appear. Her party conversation, too, with Spud, shows clichés as substitutes for real communication: the last three lines on page 57 include 'stamping ground'; 'for my sins'; 'a far-ish cry'; 'I didn't fall off the Christmas tree yesterday'.

Some of the unseen characters are apparently as unperceptive as herself. Alan Bennett gives Terry, the animal handler, a very feeble joke about mushroom growing. Lesley's reaction is unexpected, although it pinpoints the dullness underlying her pert style. She sees the joke as unsuccessful not because of its familiarity and weakness, but because it fails to take into account developments in the mushroom-growing trade. However, Nigel, the director's hard-pressed assistant, is given a trenchant style, which contrasts tellingly with Lesley's elaborate but well-worn conversational style.

There are a great many things that Lesley does not understand, including the fact that the men she meets have no difficulty in getting her into bed: the image of the cat watching the trout in Terry's bedroom is easily related **symbolically** to Gunther's subsequent seduction of the girl he has been watching as she performs nude scenes.

Muriel Carpenter's character and her circle are to some extent established by clichés which indicate the middle-class and an armed forces background. Apart from the title, *Soldiering On,* there are quite a few phrases associated with the military on the first two pages, for instance: 'coward's way out'; 'lived to fight another day'; 'staunch the flood'; 'back into the fray'; 'tackling the debris'. The other clichés which help to establish character are all well tried and – as Alan Bennett says of

his characters themselves – 'old-fashioned'. Examples among many are
'bearded him in his den'; 'a drop in the ocean'; and 'orphans of the storm'.
Alan Bennett gives Muriel other character-establishing tricks of speech.
She uses the impersonal pronoun 'one' occasionally (for example, on
p. 74, 'one would have fought tooth and nail to keep her in the private
sector), and also often uses a brisk-sounding abbreviated narrative, suited
to the style of an officer's or an executive's wife. Look, for example, at the
paragraph on page 76, beginning 'Job sorting out', which demonstrates
Muriel's memo-style communication. This is perhaps intended to
conceal emotion but, in reality, reveals it; the last page of her narrative, as
she explains how she passes her solitary days, includes a great many of
these truncated sentences.

Alone among the characters of the *Talking Heads* plays, Muriel
laughs. Susan is witty, of course, but her humour is bitter. Muriel is able
to laugh even at the funeral: when a mourner turns out to be an ex-
prisoner who has attended the funeral out of respect for Ralph, Muriel
says that she 'shrieked'. Later in the day, she and Mabel have 'a good
laugh and a good cry' over the emotional effect upon them of Ralph's
wellington boots. (See Text 3 in Textual Analysis for further detailed
commentary on a passage from this play.)

Doris has something in common with Mrs Whittaker – both are in
their seventies and both can be quite truculent, although Mrs Whittaker
is still interested in enjoying herself, whereas Doris is a prisoner of her
anxiety over the state of her house and garden. Alan Bennett has given
Doris a lively and forceful style of speech, not unlike that of Mrs
Whittaker, although Doris's narrative often betrays her lack of education:
'I never saw no list' or 'Them's her leaves', for example (p. 83). She
swears mildly, occasionally: 'oh hell, the flaming buffet' (p. 82) when
recounting the circumstances of her accident, but later uses the even less
offensive 'Oh stink'. She uses very few clichés: when she does use the
phrase 'on the carpet' (p. 84), it is with a double meaning, related to the
title, *A Cream Cracker on the Carpet*, as she sees the opportunity of an
attack on Zulema. Her speech is idiosyncratic – a mixture of the very
direct and the **colloquial** – such as 'great lolloping lamp post-smelling
articles' (p. 85) or 'graves, gardens, everything's to follow' (p. 84) – with
some unexpectedly heavyweight words like 'surreptitious' or 'gregarious'
(p. 89). Doris also uses broken sentence structure quite often; unlike

Muriel's brisk memo-like speech, Doris's often suggests something more like **stream of consciousness**, especially at the end as her thoughts wander more and more to the past.

The choice of names for the **narrators** is significant, and especially so in the case of Doris and her husband Wilfred. As she says, they are names from the past, the names of people who do not belong any more. Zulema, however, has a name which comes from a culture that Doris is not familiar with. In this play, Zulema represents authority and the present, whereas Doris knows that she and the world she remembers are finished.

The wedding photograph of Doris and Wilfred is a strong **symbol**: it has fallen from the wall as a result of Doris's endless campaign against dust, and the glass has cracked. This represents the destructive nature of Doris's cleaning mania, the loss of Wilfred – 'tidied into the grave' as Alan Bennett writes in the 'Introduction' – and, particularly, with Doris's impending death, the end of the marriage, which had continued to exist in Doris's memory.

We can see, looking at the plays both individually and as a linked group, that Alan Bennett has marshalled many different possibilities to serve his purpose in creating credible characters and stories. The convincing style of speech he has given to each narrator represents probably the most compelling means of giving them life. He also uses **parallels** in the stories and **symbolism** to underline his themes, such as, respectively, the dead children in *A Lady of Letters* and the swimming 'cossy' which has moth-holes in the bust in *Soldiering On*.

Perhaps the aspect of style and language most peculiarly his is his unerring identification of the details of everyday life that tell us so much about a person. This can refer to domestic details, to the use of familiar trade names (e.g., 'Platignum', 'Duraglit'), to clothes – often mentioned – and even to food, which features in each monologue. The menu quoted by Graham in the 'common' red café; Susan's unappetising lunch for the bishop; Miss Ruddock's hair-infested sausages; Lesley's 'fork lunch' or 'finger buffet'; Muriel's funeral feast and final boiled egg; Doris's frugal cream cracker – each of these apparently trivial references helps to pinpoint the character of the narrator or the situation. Even Alan Bennett's references to places he identifies specifically are illuminating: Scarborough and Tenerife; Spain and Lee-on-Solent; Siena and Hunstanton – these pairs of places mentioned in three of the monologues show the tastes of the characters as well as the realities of the stories. This attention to detail, the scrutiny of the minutiae of everyday life, often supplies the clues which enable us to see his narrators in the round. What his narrators talk about is, after all, as necessary to our understanding as how they speak.

PART FOUR

TEXTUAL ANALYSIS

TEXT 1   BED AMONG THE LENTILS SCENE 5 (PP. 37–8)

Come up to Susan sitting in the vestry having a cigarette. Afternoon.

You never see pictures of Jesus smiling, do you? I mentioned this to Geoffrey once. 'Good point, Susan,' is what he said, which made me wish I'd not brought it up in the first place. Said I should think of Our Lord as having an inward smile, the doctrine according to Geoffrey being that Jesus was made man so he smiled, laughed and did everything else just like the rest of us. 'Do you think he ever smirked?' I asked, whereupon Geoffrey suddenly remembered he was burying somebody in five minutes and took himself off.

If Jesus *is* all man I just wish they'd put a bit more of it into the illustrations. I was sitting in church yesterday, wrestling with this point of theology, when it occurred to me that something seemed to have happened to Geoffrey. The service should have kicked off ages ago but he's still in the vestry. Mr Bland is filling in with something uplifting on the organ and Miss Frobisher, never one to let an opportunity slip, has slumped to her knees for a spot of unscheduled silent prayer. Mrs Shrubsole is lost in contemplation of the altar, still adorned with Forest Murmurs, a trail of ivy round the cross the final inspired touch. Mr Bland now ups the volume but still no sign of Geoff. 'Arnold,' says Mrs Belcher, 'there seems to be some hiatus in the proceedings,' and suddenly the fan club is on red alert. She's just levering him to his feet when I get in first and nip in there to investigate.

His reverence is there, white-faced, every cupboard open and practically in tears. He said, 'Have you seen it?' I said, 'What?' He said, 'The wine. The communion wine. It's gone.' I said, 'That's no tragedy,' and offer to pop out and get some ordinary. Geoffrey said, 'They're not open. Besides, what does it look like?' I said, 'Well, it looks like we've run out of communion wine.' He said, 'We haven't run out. There was a full bottle here on Friday. Somebody has drunk it.'

It's on the tip of my tongue to say that if Jesus is all that he's cracked up to be why doesn't he use tap-water and put it to the test when I suddenly remember that Mr Bland keeps a bottle of cough mixture in his cupboard in case any of the choirboys gets chesty. At the thought of celebrating the Lord's Supper in Benylin Geoffrey now has a complete nervous breakdown but, as I point out, it's red and sweet and nobody is going to notice. Nor do they. I see Mr Belcher licking his lips a bit thoughtfully as he walks back down the aisle but that's all. 'What was the delay?' asks Mrs Shrubsole. 'Nothing,' I said, 'just a little hiccup.'

Having got it right for once I'm feeling quite pleased with myself, but Geoffrey obviously isn't and never speaks all afternoon so I bunk off Evensong and go into Leeds.

Mr Ramesh has evidently been expecting me because there's a bed made up in the storeroom upstairs. I go up first and get in. When I'm in bed I can put my hand out and feel the lentils running through my fingers. When he comes up he's put on his proper clothes. Long white shirt, sash and whatnot. Loincloth underneath. All spotless. Like Jesus. Only not. I watch him undress and think about them all at Evensong and Geoffrey praying in that pausy way he does, giving you time to mean each phrase. And the fan club lapping it up, thinking they love God when they just love Geoffrey. Lighten our darkness we beseech thee O Lord and by thy great mercy defend us from all perils and dangers of this night. Like Mr Ramesh who is twenty-six with lovely legs, who goes swimming every morning at Merrion Street Baths and plays hockey for Horsforth. I ask him if they offer their sex to God. He isn't very interested in the point but with them, so far as I can gather, sex is all part of God anyway. I can see why too. It's the first time I really understand what all the fuss is about. There among the lentils on the second Sunday after Trinity.

I've just popped into the vestry. He's put a lock on the cupboard door.

Go to black.

In this scene the **narrator**, Susan, is found sitting in the vestry of her husband's church, disrespectfully smoking a cigarette.

As usual in the **monologues**, we encounter the narrator in the middle of a thought sequence – there is no introductory passage. She has asked her husband, with what we take to be mock disingenuousness, why Jesus is never seen smiling. He replies, patronisingly, 'Good point, Susan,' and goes on to explain his view of Jesus in his aspect as 'man', who did everything 'just like the rest of us'. Susan is bored by his lecturing ('made me wish I'd not brought it up in the first place') and undermines Geoffrey's serious approach by asking 'Do you think he ever smirked?'

Her subversive account of life with Geoffrey continues with a cynical account of the parishioners (described by Susan as her husband's 'fan club') as they settle down in church for the Sunday morning Communion Service. Words which might normally be associated with the occasion – 'uplifting' and 'inspired' – are undercut by her parallel and flippant use of **colloquial** terms: the service 'should have kicked off'; 'a spot of prayer' is observed; the organist 'ups the volume'; 'the fan club is on red alert'. Susan manages to get to the vestry to investigate what Mrs Belcher grandly calls the 'hiatus' before Mr Belcher can be levered out of his seat. Geoffrey is panicking: the communion wine has disappeared. Susan, who knows that it is she who has drunk it, does not admit to the deed, but offers practical suggestions which ignore the solemnity of the communion ritual. She will 'pop out and get some ordinary' or, because the shops are closed, she suggests that Geoffrey use Mr Bland's cough mixture, kept in the vestry for 'chesty' choirboys. Susan's account reveals that her husband is more concerned with appearances – 'What does it look like?' – than the sanctity of his communion service. He approaches 'a complete nervous breakdown' at the thought of such a blasphemous act as 'celebrating the Lord's Supper in Benylin'; nevertheless he accepts Susan's solution to his problem. Although Susan sees Mr Belcher 'licking his lips a bit thoughtfully' as he returns to his pew, the deception succeeds. When Susan replies to Mrs Shrubsole's enquiry about the delay, 'Nothing, just a little hiccup', there is perhaps a hint of an acknowledgement that the hiccup might have been hers when she drank the wine.

Geoffrey is furious about the events of the morning, so Susan decides to 'bunk off' (a phrase associated with truanting from school) from Evensong and go and see her lover in Leeds.

Ramesh has made up a bed on the lentils in the store room above his shop. Susan is, as always, unable to escape from the Anglican turn of thought which is second nature to her. Words from the Third Collect of Anglican evening prayer, dealing with 'the perils and dangers of this night', come to her as she lies in bed. But she relishes her exotic situation as she contrasts it with mental images of Geoffrey and his parishioners at prayer in the service she has skipped. Ramesh, who makes a serious ritual of lovemaking, dresses up in his traditional white clothes to honour the occasion. There is an echo here perhaps of Geoffrey dressing in his robes for the church service – although it is Jesus to whom Susan compares Ramesh – 'Like Jesus. Only not'.

The monologue begins with the sentence: 'Geoffrey's bad enough but I'm glad I wasn't married to Jesus.' Susan has a serious quarrel with Jesus and with God, it seems; Ramesh, his religion and his practical philosophy offer her a new approach to life which she considers has its advantages. In this passage, it is the skilful lovemaking of the Hindu shopkeeper which she appreciates: 'It's the first time I really understand what all the fuss is about'.

The scene ends with Susan's observation that Geoffrey has – understandably, we might think – 'put a lock on the cupboard door'.

The informality of Susan's style is, of course, more carefully considered than it appears. Alan Bennett has created a character of some education, but her witty style seems to be reserved for the viewer or reader. We are intended to see the 'real' Susan, of course, but when she records her own conversation with Geoffrey or a parishioner it is flat or delivered in an apparently straightforward way which conceals a disingenuous purpose. To them, we are meant to guess, she must appear a somewhat drab figure, as well as a worsening alcoholic. To us, her confidantes, however – the reader or viewer – her style is highly entertaining. Unusually, she actually begins this scene with an acknowledgement of her audience – 'You never see pictures of Jesus smiling, do you?' which reinforces her conversational **tone**. She combines a vocabulary rich in slang and **colloquialisms** with a practised use of quotations from Anglican ritual – which are certainly not a comfort to her.

The generally conversational effect is created by a narrative in which there are many short sentences, some of which are broken or **loose sentences** – that is, not grammatically complete – imitating conversational narrative. There is reported speech and a less than usual amount (so far as these monologues are concerned) of recorded direct speech . The less educated narrators in *Talking Heads* have the recognisable habit of generally repeating conversations **verbatim**, including the names by which speakers address each other (as in, e.g., the reported conversation between Graham and Jackie on p. 24 of *A Chip in the Sugar*, or Lesley's determined use of the names which she 'commits to memory' in *Her Big Chance*). Susan does not have this habit and most conversations, especially with Ramesh, are reported.

Susan begins the scene in the past tense, relating her earlier conversation, when she put a theological poser to Geoffrey about Jesus's 'smirking', and continues in the past as she describes the preparations for the Sunday morning service. As the emergency arises, she moves into the present tense, which creates a more immediate effect. The rest of the scene continues in the present tense. However, Alan Bennett avoids the awkwardness in the vestry exchange between Susan and Geoffrey of 'he says' and 'I say', which has an inelegantly demotic effect. He mixes the past tense – 'he said', 'I said' – with other verbs in the present tense. In fact, Susan expresses her sense of superiority over the parishioners by using 'I said' always of her own speech, but using 'says Mrs Belcher', 'asks Mrs Shrubsole' of the speech of the parishioners she despises.

Susan remains seated throughout the scene, which helps to give continuity to her narrative. Her awkward questioning and wilfulness are evident in this scene, where she continues a story which does not tell the whole truth. Although she is not frank about it, we know by now why she has come into the vestry. She made no admission of guilt over the missing communion wine but congratulated herself on providing a solution to Geoffrey's difficulty – which after all would not have existed were it not for her clandestine drinking. The underlying story, as in all the monologues, is revealed to us by the picture that is given of the unseen characters. Here, although much of Susan's story is hilariously funny, it is difficult not to feel some sympathy for the pompous Geoffrey. He is obviously congenial enough for his parishioners to be fond of him, and his wife's total lack of sympathy for him and his vocation puts him in an unenviable position.

TEXT 2   A LADY OF LETTERS SCENE 5 (PP. 48–9)

Come up on Miss Ruddock in her hat and coat against a bare background.

Thinking about it afterwards, I realised it must have been the doctor that alerted the vicar. Came round anyway. Not the old vicar. I'd have known him. This was a young fellow in a collar and tie, could have been anybody. I didn't take the chain off. I said, 'How do I know you're the vicar, have you any identification?' He shoves a little cross round the door. I said, 'What's this?' He said, 'A cross.' I said,

'A cross doesn't mean anything. Youths wear crosses nowadays. Hooligans. They wear crosses in their ears.' He said, 'Not like this. This is a real cross. A working cross. It's the tool of my trade.' I was still a bit dubious, then I saw he had cycle clips on so I let him in.

He chats for a bit, this and that, no mention of God for long enough. They keep him up their sleeve for as long as they can, vicars, they know it puts people off. Went through a long rigmarole about love. How love comes in different forms … loving friends, loving the countryside, loving music. People would be surprised to learn, he said (and I thought, 'Here we go'), people would be surprised to learn that they loved God all the time and just didn't know it. I cut him short. I said, 'If you've come round here to talk about God you're barking up the wrong tree. I'm an atheist.' He was a bit stumped, I could see. They don't expect you to be an atheist when you're a miss. Vicars, they think if you're a single person they're on a good wicket. He said, 'Well, Miss Ruddock, I shall call again. I shall look on you as a challenge.'

He hadn't been gone long when there's another knock, only this time it's a policeman, with a woman policeman in tow. Ask if they can come in and have a word. I said, 'What for?' He said, 'You know what for.' I said, 'I don't,' but I let them in. Takes his helmet off, only young and says he'll come straight to the point: was it me who'd been writing these letters? I said, 'What letters? I don't write letters.' He said, 'Letters.' I said, 'Everyone writes letters. I bet you write letters.' He said, 'Not like you, love.' I said, 'Don't love me. You'd better give me your name and number. I intend to write to your superintendent.'

It turns out it's to do with the couple opposite. I said, 'Well, why are you asking me?' He said, 'We're asking you because who was it wrote to the chemist saying his wife was a prostitute? We're asking you because who was it gave the lollipop man a nervous breakdown?' I said, 'Well, he was interfering with those children.' He said, 'The court bound you over to keep the peace. This is a serious matter.' I said, 'It is a serious matter. I can't keep the peace when there's cruelty and neglect going on under my nose. I shouldn't keep the peace when there's a child suffering. It's not my duty to keep the peace then, is it?' So then madam takes over, the understanding approach. She said didn't I appreciate this was a caring young couple? I said if they were a caring young couple why did you never see the kiddy? If they were a caring young couple why did they go gadding off every night, leaving the kiddy alone in the house? She said because the kiddy wasn't alone in the house. The kiddy wasn't in the house. The kiddy was in hospital in Bradford, that's where they were going every night. And that's where the kiddy died, last Friday. I said, 'What of? Neglect?' She said, 'No. Leukaemia.'

Pause.

He said, 'You'd better get your hat and coat on.'

Go to black.

In the previous scene Miss Ruddock has been to see a doctor at her local practice, so the explanation she gives of the vicar's reason for visiting her – 'alerted by the doctor' – is logical.

Miss Ruddock sees her life as full of regrettable changes, and it is no surprise that the vicar, too, has changed. 'I'd have known him,' she says of the 'old vicar'. She notes that her visitor is informally dressed – 'a young fellow in a collar and tie' and claims to be unsure whether or not he is a vicar. He offers a cross as identification, which she rejects, pointing out with some acerbity that 'Youths wear crosses nowadays. Hooligans. They wear crosses in their ears.' It is not his so-called 'working cross' which convinces her, she says, but the fact that he must be making his visits on a bicycle, since he is wearing cycle clips.

Miss Ruddock, who has apparently heard it all before, listens with some disdain to what the vicar has to say – 'a long rigmarole' – and waits for the inevitable reference to God – (and I thought, 'Here it comes'). She triumphantly halts him with the unexpected statement, '"I am an atheist."' She uses a cricketing image to emphasise her success in what she has treated as something of a contest – 'He was a bit stumped, I could see' – and extends her sporting **metaphor** with reference to vicars thinking 'they're on a good wicket' when they are dealing with a single woman, 'a miss'.

Miss Ruddock's next visitors are a policeman and policewoman. They have come to ask about her letter writing. The doughty Miss Ruddock is a little flustered, we guess, because she contradicts herself. 'What letters? I don't write letters,' she says, followed by the admission, 'Everyone writes letters. I bet you write letters.' The policeman addresses her informally as 'love', which gives Miss Ruddock, offended, a chance to ask for his name and number. She gives away her tendency to write a letter on the smallest pretext by saying, 'I intend to write to your superintendent.'

Alan Bennett has taken care to prepare the ground to some extent, but it is still a surprise to discover that Miss Ruddock has been involved in criminal activity by writing libellous letters about the chemist's wife and the local lollipop-man; she has already been to court and has been bound over to keep the peace.

The police are here because she has written a letter accusing the young couple opposite of neglecting their child. Miss Ruddock defends herself stoutly to the police woman, listing her deductions about the young couple's apparently unsatisfactory behaviour. The police woman, in a devastating sequence, explains how wrong Miss Ruddock had been and that the couple had not been 'gadding off' at night, but visiting their terminally sick child. The child had died in hospital. Miss Ruddock battles on, asking defiantly, 'What of? Neglect?'

When the policewoman tells her that the child in fact died of leukaemia, Miss Ruddock does not acknowledge that she has been in any way at fault, but the 'pause' indicated serves to show that she is reflecting on what has happened, before she says that she was told to put on her outdoor clothes.

As in all the **monologues**, the **narrator**'s style is informal and conversational, with many short and incomplete sentences, which suggest Miss Ruddock is voicing her thoughts as they come to her and describing the visits of the vicar and the police as they happened. Her vocabulary has been established at some time well in the past, it seems, and Alan Bennett has given her some rather old-fashioned expressions in this passage, such as: 'They keep him up their sleeve', 'barking up the wrong tree' and the cricketing **metaphors** already mentioned. The term 'kiddy' for child, too, was more popular in the past.

But what is particularly typical of Miss Ruddock is her combative style. She is openly aggressive to the vicar and dismisses what she sees as his predictable 'rigmarole' about love in a scornful summary. She is equally aggressive in her reaction to the police, defending herself fiercely. The policeman – like the vicar – is 'only young', presumably not a point in his favour. She manages to express her disapproval of the policewoman

by describing her as 'a woman policeman in tow', suggesting she sees her
as a somewhat freakish figure; Miss Ruddock's later reference to her as
'madam' is certainly not deferential, and she identifies the way in which
the policewoman adopts 'the understanding approach' as a professional
device.

We realise that Miss Ruddock's misconceptions about her various
neighbours could have been cleared up had she been able to communicate
verbally with them, but this she has been unable to do. In fact, Miss
Ruddock is very much alone and, unusually in *Talking Heads*, there are no
conversations to be recorded in the first three scenes of the play. In scene
four, before the passage above, Miss Ruddock does give exchanges with
two different doctors in direct speech, as well as some reported speech.
However, in the key scene five, above, much of the conversation with the
vicar owes its humour to being presented in direct speech, as though it
were a **verbatim** account. The interview with the police, which provides
one of the dramatic highlights of the play, is also necessarily in direct
speech, with only brief linking narrative. This, apart from underlining the
drama of the situation, also offers Miss Ruddock the opportunity to avoid
comment upon the accusations which are made against her. Alan Bennett
uses an interesting device at the end of the police visit, when the
policewoman's explanation of what has happened is given not quite in
direct speech. Although the words given could be those actually spoken
by the policewoman, we may think – because of the repeated use of Miss
Ruddock's term 'the kiddy' – that this is the narrator's reworking of what
was said. In any case, the sequence of four sentences, with 'the kiddy'
repeated in each one as the subject, is an effective way of building up
tension to the final statement, 'And that's where the kiddy died, last
Friday'.

We have had hints about Miss Ruddock 'getting a bit upset' and
we know her penchant for letter writing. Nevertheless, it is clear that,
like the other narrators of *Talking Heads*, Miss Ruddock has been giving
us a very incomplete account of events in the previous scenes. The
shock of the police disclosure of the less innocent aspect of her letter
writing is to some extent prepared for by the fact that she is sitting 'in
her hat and coat against a bare background' – presumably at the police
station or at the social services offices. This alerts us to the possibility
of a dramatic change by her displacement from her sitting room and

the bay window, from which she makes her deluded assessments of what her neighbours are up to.

TEXT 3   SOLDIERING ON SCENE 2 (PP. 72–3)

Come up on Muriel sitting in an armchair. Evening.

Everybody I run into says not to take any big decisions. I staggered into the Community Centre bearing Ralph's entire wardrobe which Angela Gillespie had nipped in smartish and earmarked for Muscular Dystrophy. Five minutes later, Brenda Bousfield had come knocking at the door on behalf of Cystic Fibrosis. Knives out straight away, I practically had to separate them. In fact I did separate them in the end, the City suits to Angela and Brenda the tweeds. All lovely stuff. Beautiful dinner jacket from Hawes and Curtis, done for Giles if he hadn't got so fat. Mind you, he didn't want the ties either. Angela did. 'Lovely jumble,' she said. 'How're you coping? Don't take any big decisions, one day at a time, I don't use any shoes.'

Actually I'd been silly and kept his shoes back. I loved his shoes. Always used to clean them. 'My shoeshine lady.' 'Whatever you do,' Angela said, 'don't give them to Brenda. They're top heavy on staff, their group, it's well-known. It all goes on the admin. We can use shoes.'

I thought I'd go into the library and see if Miss Dunsmore could find me something on bereavement. That's something I learned from Ralph: plug into other people's experience, pool your resources. 'A new experience is like travelling through unknown country. But remember, others have taken this road before you, old girl, and left notes. So Question no. 1: Is there a map? Question no. 2: Am I taking advantage of all the information available? It doesn't matter if you're going to get married, commit a burglary or keep a guinea pig; efficiency is the proper collation of information.' Oh Ralph.

Miss Dunsmore did a reconnoitre round, but the only information she could come up with was a book about burial customs in Papua New Guinea. I think even Ralph would draw the line at that. However, she thought the Health Centre did a pamphlet on bereavement. Miss Dunsmore said she wasn't offering this as consolation but apparently elephants go into mourning and so, very strangely, does the pike. So we chatted about that for a bit. Told me not to take any big decisions, and if I was throwing away any of his books could I steer them her way as she ran some sort of reading service for the disabled.

I dropped into the Health Centre and the receptionist said there was a pamphlet on death; they'd had some on the counter, only the tots kept taking them to scribble on, so they hadn't re-ordered. She said she'd skimmed through it and the gist of it was not to take any big decisions and to throw yourself into something. I said, 'You don't mean the canal?' She said, 'Come again?' Nobody expects you to make jokes. As I was going out she called me back and said did Ralph wear spectacles? Because if he did, not to throw away the old pairs as owing to cutbacks they'd started a spectacles recycling scheme.

Back at base Mabel said Margaret had been plonked on the chair in the passage all morning with her bag packed and her outside coat on, and for some reason wellington boots. Said the police were coming. We manhandled her upstairs, and after about seventeen goes I managed to smuggle in a tablet which did the trick and she'd just settled down for a little zizz when who should draw up at the door but Giles.

He'd cancelled all his appointments, eluded the guards at the office and just belted down the A12 because he suddenly thought I might need cheering up, bless him. He could always get round Mabel ever since he was little, so she agrees to hold the fort while he whisks me off to lunch at somewhere rather swish. I thought to myself, I hope you're watching, Ralph, you old rascal, and eating your words. Ralph and Giles never got on for more than five minutes whereas, it's funny, he was always dotty about Mags.

In this first part of the second scene of the **monologue**, Muriel is trying to tackle some practical tasks resulting from her husband's death. She has no trouble disposing of Ralph's personal belongings – her friends Angela Gillespie and Brenda Bousfield, both voluntary workers for different charities, descend upon her and compete for Ralph's clothes. 'I practically had to separate them,' Muriel says, surprised at the intensity of their rivalry. Angela admires the ties she is given – 'Lovely jumble' – and offers a perfunctory enquiry about Muriel herself: 'How're you coping? Don't take any big decisions, one day at a time,' she advises, asking in the same breath about Ralph's shoes, which she does not want to go to Brenda's charity because, she claims 'It all goes on the admin'.

Muriel had not wanted to part with Ralph's shoes, which she always used to clean. Ralph called her his 'shoeshine lady', she remembers.

She remembers too how Ralph taught her to deal with new experiences, to find out what appropriate information is available and to take advantage of it. As she re-enacts Ralph's formula, ending "'Efficiency is the proper collation of information'", which she has obviously heard more than once, she is as near as she will ever get to breaking down – 'Oh Ralph'.

Miss Dunsmore at the library is not a great deal of help in Muriel's quest for information about how to tackle bereavement. She can find only 'a book about burial customs in Papua New Guinea'; well-meaning, but at a loss for something to say, she tells Muriel, incongruously, about the mourning habits of elephants and the pike. She, too, advises Muriel to take no big decisions and asks if she can have any of Ralph's books which Muriel might be discarding for her reading service for the disabled. At the Health Centre they have run out of pamphlets on death: 'the tots kept taking them to scribble on' Muriel is told, the statement underlining a lack of respect for death and the needs of the bereaved with an **irony** which is obvious neither to Muriel nor the receptionist. Again there is a request – this time for Ralph's spectacles for recycling – and what is obviously the standard advice to take no big decisions. The receptionist suggests that Muriel should throw herself into something, but is unable to respond to Muriel's brave joke about throwing herself into the canal – 'Nobody expects you to make jokes'.

At home, Muriel's housekeeper Mabel says that Margaret has been 'plonked on the chair in the passage' for some time, with her coat and wellington boots on, suitcase packed, and under the impression that the police were coming. It is clear from the first scene that Muriel's daughter is ill and here Muriel and Mabel are obviously used to her delusions and get her to bed and sedated – not without a good deal of difficulty, since she has to be 'manhandled' upstairs and it takes 'about seventeen goes' to get her to swallow a tablet.

Finally in this passage, Muriel's adored son Giles appears to take her out to lunch, 'somewhere rather swish'. Muriel is taken in by Giles's apparent concern for her, but we understand that his father had a poor opinion of their son, which he must have voiced, since Muriel thinks that he would have to 'eat his words' now. 'They never got on for more than five minutes', we learn, although of course he was 'always dotty' about his daughter. The dislike was mutual, then, and explains why Giles did not want to take any of his father's personal possessions.

The narrative follows the usual pattern in *Talking Heads* which sustains a conversational style; there are many short and truncated sentences. Muriel goes over the events of the day, and her thoughts wander between the practical tasks which she has undertaken and her memories of Ralph. Even in this ruminative mood her style is quite brisk and amusing; her fortitude is evident, even so soon after her bereavement. The vocabulary that Alan Bennett has given her could be described as a blend of the schoolgirlish and the military. She has been an army wife and she repeats **verbatim** Ralph's recommendation to 'plug into other people's experiences, pool your resources', delivering his 'Question no. 1' and 'Question no. 2' in the style of a military briefing. Other military language appears, as it does throughout the **monologue**: Miss Dunsmore does a 'reconnoitre' around; Mabel is 'back at base'; Giles has 'eluded the guards' and Mabel agrees to 'hold the fort'. Something of a military style 'memo' construction is evident, too, from time to time in the monologue. There is an example of this note-like effect in the first paragraph: 'All lovely stuff. Beautiful dinner jacket from Hawes and Curtis, done for Giles if he hadn't got so fat'.

However, the slangy, emphatic vocabulary which enlivens her narrative has probably been hers since school days. She 'staggered' into the Community Centre; Angela 'nipped in'; Margaret had been 'plonked on the chair'; it took Muriel 'about seventeen goes' to administer medication; Margaret settled for 'a little zizz'; Giles 'just belted down the A12'; Ralph was 'dotty about Mags'.

In this passage, Muriel is looking for guidance, but finds little. She has certainly faced up to changes of circumstances before – Ralph had 'touched life at many points' we learned in Scene 1, and no doubt Muriel was beside him during all the aspects of his career. She does not lack the will to organise her new life, but she receives little help other than the many times reiterated advice to take no big decisions (which of course she promptly forgets when Giles gets to work on her later). It is **ironic**, especially as the play draws to its bleak conclusion, that the voluntary workers who form a large part of her circle and who expend so much energy on support for the unfortunate, are not able to recognise a need within their midst.

The *Talking Heads* monologues are all quite heavily plotted, but the clues and hints which drive the story forward are introduced unobtrusively. We already know that Margaret is ill and there seems to be little affection between her and her mother; here Muriel describes the difficulties of getting Margaret to bed in detached and practical terms, and no feeling for her daughter is evident. Giles, however, is obviously her favourite. In this scene, the seeds of the resolution of the narrative are sown. Margaret's illness, it is becoming clearer, is associated with her father and we guess that she feels – in her confusion – that she is in some way responsible for his death. We note, too, that her father was 'always dotty about Mags'. Later in the scene, Giles persuades his mother to begin the process of signing away her capital. And, in the passage above, we begin to wonder about Giles's motives when we learn that he can 'get round' Mabel as we see he 'gets round' Muriel.

These revelations, however, about Giles's fraud and Ralph's abuse of his daughter, are yet to come. Here, the **narrator's** character is firmly established. Muriel, of course, unlike any of the other *Talking Heads*, is a prosperous and socially adept member of the middle-class. She expects to be able to manage her life successfully. She meets her husband's death with fortitude and without losing her sense of humour. She seems admirable. But, as with all the other monologues, there is another story emerging behind what the narrator tells us. Muriel is a woman who knows how to run a large household well enough, but it is becoming clear that she does not really know the members of her family. We begin to understand that the real story she has to tell is about her misreading of events past and present, and her faulty perception of the natures of her husband and son.

PART FIVE

BACKGROUND

ALAN BENNETT

EARLY YEARS

Alan Bennett was born in 1934 in Yorkshire and – in spite of the cosmopolitan nature of much of his later life – he is still very much a northerner. He was the second of the two sons of a butcher who worked for the local 'Co-op' (Co-operative Society) in Leeds, where Alan Bennett grew up. The Second World War broke out when he was five and his childhood and early teenage years were, like those of most of his contemporaries, spent living through austere, disciplined times, with food and clothing rationed. He attended the local Upper Armley National School, followed by Leeds Modern School. By his own account, he was a shy, bookish child, and fervently religious in his teens. When he left school, it was with the offer of a place at Sydney Sussex College, Cambridge. However, two years compulsory National Service intervened and he was sent – first to Bodmin in Cornwall and then to Cambridge – on the Joint Services Language Course to learn Russian, in the early days of the Cold War. Having enjoyed a taste of university life at Cambridge, he decided to try for Oxford, and succeeded in gaining an Open Scholarship in history at Exeter College.

Too self-conscious as a student to join OUDS (the Oxford University Dramatic Society) or the Experimental Theatre Club, Alan Bennett nevertheless found his way to dramatic success through the end of term junior common room smoking concerts. These were, he writes, 'uproarious drunken affairs ... in the direct line of those camp concerts POWs (prisoners of war) spent their time in acting when they weren't busy tunnelling under the foundations' (*Writing Home*, 1994, p. 18). For one of these concerts, Alan Bennett wrote a **parody** of an Anglican vicar's sermon, a form with which he was very familiar.

This 'sermon' (now said to be on the syllabus of several theological courses) was very successful at the Edinburgh Festival Fringe and its highly favourable reception in fact earned Alan Bennett a place in the celebrated satirical revue *Beyond the Fringe* the following year. He and Dudley Moore, another Oxford student, together with Jonathan Miller and Peter Cook, from Cambridge, were invited to put together the original version of *Beyond the Fringe* as an official Edinburgh Festival revue in 1960. *Beyond the Fringe* enjoyed a run in London's West End the following year and went on Broadway in New York in 1962.

By this time Alan Bennett was a postgraduate at Oxford (having researched 'Richard II's retinue from 1388 to 1399'), and was working as a temporary tutor in history at Exeter and Magdalen Colleges. He did not enjoy teaching, finding it so difficult to produce enough discussion points to fill the tuition hours, he claims, that he resorted to putting the clock forward before tutorials. He hoped that 'the celebrity of the revue to some degree compensated my pupils for the shortcomings of the tuition' (*Writing Home*, 1994, p. 21).

ALAN BENNETT'S WORK

Since his brilliant success in *Beyond the Fringe*, which was a turning point in his career, Alan Bennett has often acted and sometimes directed but his primary concern has been with writing for the stage and television. He has written over twenty plays, his stage plays including the satirical comedies *Forty Years On* (produced in 1968), *Getting On* (1971) and *Habeas Corpus* (1973). *The Old Country* (1977), a darker work, is concerned with the life of an English spy in what used to be the Soviet Union and his decision whether or not to return to an England that has radically changed. His most recent stage successes have been a new version of *The Wind in the Willows*, first performed at the Royal National Theatre in 1990, and *The Madness of George III*, first performed at the same theatre in 1991, and later made into a film as *The Madness of King George*. His published work for television consists of groups of plays, published under the titles *Objects of Affection and Other Plays for Television* (BBC, 1984), *The Writer in Disguise* (Faber, 1985), *Two* Kafka *Plays* (Faber, 1987), *Talking Heads* (BBC, 1988) and *Single Spies* (Faber, 1989). A second series of *Talking Heads* was screened on BBC2 in 1998. In 1994, Alan Bennett published *Writing Home*, which was selected by many critics as their 'book of the year'. This is an often funny and sometimes touching collection of talks, diaries and occasional journalism, much of it

written in his idiosyncratic, oblique style, and containing as much
information as he cares to reveal about his life and the sources of his
material.

'Speaking properly' and 'being yourself'

Alan Bennett sees a division in his view of the world, brought about by
growing up in the provinces and living his adult life mainly in London.
He is conscious of 'an anxiety about sincerity' in the way he writes. He
illustrates what he thinks is a split in his literary integrity by what, in the
'Introduction' to *Writing Home* (1994), he describes as the 'parable' of his
mother's chance meeting with T.S. Eliot. In his work as a butcher, Alan
Bennett's father's customers included a Mrs Fletcher, whose daughter
Valerie became the second wife of the great poet. One day, Mrs Bennett
met Mrs Fletcher in the street with her son-in-law, and introductions
were made. Mrs Bennett had met and spoken to the famous poet, T.S.
Eliot, although at the time she was completely unaware of his literary
significance. Alan Bennett explains that for him this meeting
encompassed an image of how, when he began to write, it was in 'two
different voices', a metropolitan voice – 'speaking properly' – and a
provincial voice – 'being yourself'. T.S. Eliot represented Art, Culture
and Literature, written with capital letters and to do with 'speaking
properly', and his mother represented life, 'resolutely,' as he says, 'in the
lower case', and concerned with 'being yourself'.

In his first work, his sketches for revues and his stage plays, Alan
Bennett wrote with what he claims was an assumed voice, the voice that
he had met in novels or at Sunday matinees at the local theatre –
'metropolitan, literary and middle-class'. His first attempt at 'being
himself' and using his 'Northern voice' was, he writes, a complete failure.
In a refurbished version of *Beyond the Fringe* on Broadway in 1963, one
of his new sketches was a humorous **monologue** about death, as it might
be viewed in the North of England. This was a topic that was somewhat
taboo at that time, especially as a subject for humour, and the setting of
the North of England was almost guaranteed to be incomprehensible to
a New York audience.

Alan Bennett says that 'it's in the process of imitating the voices
of others that one comes to learn the sound of one's own' (*Writing*

Home, 1994, xii). He feels that the dichotomy of metropolitan and provincial still persists. He has found that for him, as a general rule, his personal voice – the voice he was born with – has been most suited to his television plays. In any case, he has come to the conclusion that, for a writer these days, having two voices is 'more a worry about consistency' than a serious problem.

The reader or viewer of *Talking Heads* will recognise that in most of the monologues Alan Bennett is 'being himself' and, as he puts it, using the voice with which he was born. And it is clear that much of his material has been plundered from his past. He claims, like the poet Philip Larkin (1922–85), that his childhood was 'unspent' in a provincial city, and that life – which did not 'live up to literature' – was something that happened elsewhere. His parents were diffident people, feeling that their lack of confidence was due to inadequate education. Alan Bennett does not concur with this view, insisting that even his extended education failed to make him a confident figure in the world. Wartime shortages and the failure of life to come up to the standard of children's stories, with their expansive, middle-class, country backgrounds and frequent adventures, left him with a sense of disappointment. The ordinariness of his childhood meant that he could claim neither to have been privileged nor deprived.

Nevertheless, if life in Leeds could not be lived on a grand scale of adventure or wretchedness, it proved a training ground for those skills which can be associated with Alan Bennett's short television plays, and particularly *Talking Heads*. If there is one characteristic in particular which marks Alan Bennett's work as a dramatist, it is his acute ear for the nuances of everyday speech. This dates from his Leeds days, as does his recreation of those formidable northern women who figure in several of the monologues.

Although an actor who can assume many personae, Alan Bennett, as himself, is a familiar figure on the television screen, and he has perhaps resolved his supposed problem of the division between his 'metropolitan' self and his 'provincial' self. As a guide around Westminster Abbey in a series of three television programmes first shown over the Christmas period of 1995, he was certainly 'being himself'. His familiar indecisive agonising, and his confident historian's familiarity with the Abbey, seemed to be equally parts of the one person. His often amusing but

LITERARY BACKGROUND   BACKGROUND

ALAN BENNETT continued

always straight-faced commentary, with its occasional melancholy overtones, was typical, too, of the writer or – at least – of the face he chooses to show the public.

L ITERARY BACKGROUND

Just as the characters and themes of *Talking Heads* seem to belong to an earlier period (see Political and Social Background) so the plays, too, seem to have little in common with the stylistic literary preoccupations of the Eighties. In spite of the frequently predicted death of the novel, it continued to flourish in a period of experimentation in what has been called the 'aftermath' of Modernism, which developed in the early part of the century. Writing in *The Modern British Novel* (Penguin, 1993) Malcolm Bradbury claims (p. 458) that, following the Eighties, contemporary fiction routinely involves:

apocalyptic cities, serial killers, gender wars, feminist self-discoveries, marital collapse, familial disintegration, child abuse, alien visitations, dark prospects and embittered shapeless lives. There are constant bitter battles of generation, gender, class, ethnic and regional identity, new wars over representation, all presided over by an anxious atmosphere of disorder, terror or gothic extremity.

He no doubt has many writers in mind, who might include – to take a few very varied examples from key figures of the Eighties – Martin Amis, Graham Swift, Fay Weldon, Salman Rushdie, Jeanette Winterson and Roddy Doyle.

Echoes of some of the themes listed by Malcolm Bradbury may be heard in *Talking Heads*, but, when we consider his style in relation to the short story format which the plays approximate, it is clear that he has little to do with the typical end-of-the-century modes, which tend towards hybridisation (or the mixing of genres), sketchiness, chronological fragmentation and open-endedness. Some of these characteristics would be found, for instance, in the short stories of Angela Carter or Ian McEwen. Alan Bennett's monologues, seen as short stories, belong to a more traditional form, with clearly developing characterisation, precise time scales and a heavily plotted structure.

As plays, equally, the style is traditional rather than innovative, except for the ambitious use of monologue form (see Tragicomedy in

Part Three). However, in an important sense, *Talking Heads* belongs absolutely to the late Eighties. The plays are very much part of television drama developments of that period. There was much shaking of heads among dramatists and critics over the dwindling amount of time given to single plays in Eighties television. Alan Bennett himself had contributed several highly successful examples – five, for instance, in 1982 (see Background – Alan Bennett). But, in the ratings wars which were raging, TV channels had identified a need to build up regular audiences; this led to a proliferation of series and serial drama – and of course to the development of new 'soaps', which were to confront the contemporary issues of society: *Brookside* from 1982 and *EastEnders* from 1985.

Drama serials flourished, too. Particularly memorable among many are the bitter comedy serial, *Boys From the Black Stuff* (1982), by Alan Bleasdale and the political thriller by Troy Kennedy Martin, *Edge of Darkness* (1985). Paul Scott's four novels, known as the Raj Quartet, provided the material for a colonial costume dramatisation, *The Jewel in the Crown* (1984). Then there were the series, which included *Talking Heads* as well as the *Inspector Morse* (1987 on) plays, based on Colin Dexter's detective stories, and the comic realist *Yes, Minister* (1980–5) and *Yes, Prime Minister* (1986–8). The 'soaps', of course, have the advantage – from the point of view of retaining a loyal audience – that they never end, but all these other successful productions, too, different as they are, met the need for drama presented in series or serials. Alan Bennett's six forty-minute plays fitted the pattern well. He writes that he had to insist on a favourable 'slot' for *Talking Heads,* which he identified as Sunday evening, and the plays were a popular and critical success. In his monologues, he had found a dramatic format to which – given his unique gift for **tragicomedy** – television was ideally suited, which was inexpensive to make, and which exploited the skills of some of our most talented actors.

T HE EIGHTIES AND BEFORE – SOCIAL AND
POLITICAL BACKGROUND

The Eighties represented a period of some national drama. Britain engaged in the Falklands War; there was an extended and acrimonious miners' strike which divided the nation's sympathies; unemployment rose – and fell; Britain hesitated about joining the European Exchange Rate (ERM); and the hated Poll Tax was established. It was, above all, the era of the ascendency of Mrs Thatcher's government, with her election victories of 1983 and 1987, and a period in which she claimed to have 'changed everything'.

If there is no reference to any of these events in *Talking Heads*, written in 1987, it is because these are very intimate and domestic plays. It is private and not public problems that matter here – the wider world does not impinge on the ordinary lives of Alan Bennett's **narrators**. They are also, as he has agreed, rather old-fashioned characters that he has created. They are contemporary with the Eighties but hardly up to date, except perhaps in the case of Lesley in *Her Big Chance*, whose experience does suggest the period.

There are topical references, however, such as Graham's to the self-help 'Community Caring' group, Miss Ruddock's to the 'hooligans" fashion for wearing crosses in the ears, or Susan's to the 'Forest Murmurs' 'school of thought' in flower arranging. These references are not made with any sense of approval, however. In fact, most of the narrators of the monologues are conscious of changes which they deplore. The past was perceived as better, it seems, in many cases. It is not the Eighties which are influential here, but earlier decades of the century in which some of the characters formed their attitudes to life.

The years after the Second World War, the Fifties and especially the Sixties, witnessed dramatic changes in the structure of society, against which many of Alan Bennett's characters are still reacting. Until the post-war years, especially in the provinces where lifestyles changed only slowly, the Church was held in high esteem and the clergy in local communities were genuinely respected figures. Also respected were the elderly and, as there was relatively little social mobility, families – especially working-class ones – were more closely knit; the elderly were not expected to live in isolation, and neighbours were far more knowledgeable about each other's lives and in many cases more supportive. Girls were expected to marry, and were brought up to think that sex before marriage was wrong, which is not to say that it did not take place, but it was certainly secretive and little discussed in public. It was still a hierarchical society with a firm – many would say rigid – structure. The 1960s, with an explosion of free love, anarchic values and a focus on youth, changed all that for good. The feeling of release from stifling traditional constraints made it an exciting time to live through for the young, but it is clear that Alan Bennett's characters are not children of the Sixties in any sense. Most are too old, in any case, but even Graham and Susan, for instance, seem to have been moulded by older traditions.

If it is society, through the National Health Service and the social services, that is trying, in the Eighties, to meet some of the problems of the narrators, they are not necessarily grateful. Although Graham appreciates Dr Chaudhury's support, Miss Ruddock puts her medication down the lavatory; social workers are made fun of more than once; Doris would sooner die than go to the old people's home that is society's response to her need. The Church's attempts, as well, to meet the needs of parishioners are scorned in several of the monologues.

Britain has become a multi-cultural society, and this is a cause of puzzlement or anxiety to some of the characters: in *A Chip in the Sugar,* Frank Turnbull makes racist remarks, whilst Mrs Whittaker believes her magazine from the Asian newsagent smells of curry. For Susan, however, her unexpected encounter with Hindu culture is revelatory, and Muriel is mildly interested to discuss religion with a follower of the Hare Krishna cult. Doris's sensible home help, exotically named Zulema, sounds as though she might be from the West Indies: at the end of her narrative, Doris comments on the way in which the more familiar names of her generation now belong only to those ripe for old people's homes.

PART SIX

CRITICAL HISTORY AND BROADER PERSPECTIVES

The *Talking Heads* series was very well received by the press when the monologues were first screened in 1987. Praise for Alan Bennett's technique and interest in his subject matter was widespread, with scarcely a dissenting voice.

He was of course by this time a celebrated writer of both stage and television plays. A previous sequence of plays in 1982, mostly collected in *Objects of Affection and Other Plays for TV* (BBC, 1982) in particular can be seen as anticipating the developments of *Talking Heads*. Madeleine Kingsley, writing in an interview with Alan Bennett in the *Radio Times* (6–12 November, 1982), suggested that his acute observation of everyday detail gave 'his new, but so familiarly *droll*, scripts a natural unity as the minutely-observed, wholly humdrum social history of a passing, usually Northern English, breed.' She continues, 'Without Alan Bennett we should know they existed, but we might not actually want to meet, to laugh at and to care about the plethora of "ladies in little costumes" who people his plays'.

Peggy Schofield, 'the archetypal senior spinster secretary', is the narrator of the monologue *A Woman of No Importance* (first performed in 1982), which is a clear forerunner of the *Talking Heads* plays. Of her, Madeleine Kingsley says 'she's the office bore you'd cross the canteen to avoid, without Alan Bennett's devastatingly authentic pen to hold you spellbound throughout her astonishing 47-minute monologue'. The praise for this particular play, with the talented Patricia Routledge in the role of Miss Schofield, must have been encouragement for Alan Bennett to proceed later with his dramatically daring enterprise of a whole series of one character plays.

Madeleine Kingsley used the word 'droll' ('oddly or strangely amusing' OED) appreciatively of Alan Bennett's work in 1982, but in 1988, the critic Peter Lennon described Alan Bennett's creations as 'quaint' ('piquantly or attractively unfamiliar, or old-fashioned', OED) in a pejorative sense. Lennon begins his review in *The Listener* (now defunct), of 28 April, 1988, with high praise for Alan Bennett, referring to 'his ability to make you see a person and glimpse his or her state of mind by the use of telling little turns of phrase, which is the gift of the expert gossip'. He goes on to describe the beginnings of feelings of unease which he experiences as the monologues proceed. The narrators, he says, 'are not quite caricatures, but their quaintness more than their humanity predominates'. He then briefly makes out a case for a rather devastating criticism of what he sees as overplotting in the monologues: the narrators 'are trapped in something. You don't realise what it is until the end. Then you realise that they are trapped in a banal anecdote; fabricated for an anecdote, which is Alan Bennett's great weakness. He has to round it off with punchlines of predictable triteness'.

There may be something to be said for the criticism that Alan Bennett's monologues carry too great a weight of plot for their structure, but certainly the great majority of reviewers' commentaries have been highly appreciative. Popular interest, of course, has centred on the dramatist himself as much as on his work; although Alan Bennett is a discreet celebrity, he has let us know something of himself and his life in his autobiographical *Writing Home* (Faber, 1994).

There has been, as yet, little extended academic assessment of Alan Bennett's work, although there is an essay in *British Television Drama in the 1980s* (George W. Brandt, ed., 1993), focusing on *A Bed Among the Lentils*. The author of this essay, Albert Hunt, discusses the making of the monologue and in particular Maggie Smith's interpretation of the role of Susan.

The most substantial commentary so far has come from Daphne Turner, in *Alan Bennett: In a Manner of Speaking* (Faber, 1997). She includes a chapter on *Talking Heads* in which there are some helpful comments on the nature of stereotyping, and on the voices which Alan Bennett gives to some of society's marginalised members. It seems, however, that Alan Bennett's work generally has eluded the probings of contemporary critical approaches. It might have been expected, for instance, that there would have been some feminist interpretations of Alan Bennett's presentation in society of his many female characters in *Talking Heads*, or that post-structuralists would have examined the plays with the tools of deconstruction.

However, shrewd as many of Alan Bennett's insights are, these are not weighty works, and may have escaped scrutiny on the grounds that they are primarily entertainment. There is a sense, too, in which critical comment is already 'written in' by Alan Bennett himself, and which the viewer or reader is invited to share. No feminist would deny that we can clearly see that the varying forms of femininity on show in *Talking Heads* are presented as constructs of society. Taking deconstruction at its most basic level, as an examination of the **subtext**, Alan Bennett already lays the trail for us, and invites us to search for a reading which is beyond what the narrator has to tell. This is what makes the monologues so fascinating. Deconstruction at a further level might find us, as readers and 'observers', in disturbing territory, in which we share the amused – if compassionate – detachment of the writer: however, at the same time, we might be forced to consider not only the narrators' status in society, but also our own acceptance of a society which suits us but not them.

FURTHER READING

ALAN BENNETT'S WORK

Apart from the *Talking Heads* collection, a good deal of Alan Bennett's dramatic work has been published, as follows:

BBC Books, London:

Forty Years On, 1969
Getting On, 1972
The Old Country, 1978
Office Suite, 1981
Objects of Affection and Other Plays for TV, 1982 (revised 1984)

Faber, London:

The Writer in Disguise, 1985
Two Kafka Plays (The Insurance Man and *Kafka's Dick),* 1987
Single Spies, 1989
The Madness of George III, 1992

Of particular interest for background material is Alan Bennett's highly successful autobiographical collection of essays, diaries and reviews, *Writing Home,* published by Faber in 1994. This includes the fascinating

Lady in the Van, an account of the life of a homeless woman who lived in his London garden for fifteen years.

The Clothes They Stood Up In, which Alan Bennett calls 'A Story', originally appeared in the *London Review of Books*, 28 November, 1996, and has subsequently been published in small paperback format by Profile Books, 1998.

CRITICAL WRITING

Daphne Turner has written a study of Alan Bennett's writing 'in relation to the man and his background'. This is *Alan Bennett: In a Manner of Speaking*, Faber, 1997, and it includes a chapter on *Talking Heads*.

There is an essay on *Bed Among the Lentils* by Albert Hunt, in *British Television Drama in the 1980s*, George W. Brandt, ed., Cambridge University Press, 1993.

If you have access to a newspaper library, you will be able to look up the articles quoted briefly in Part Six, Critical History; the presentation of the new series of *Talking Heads* on BBC television, autumn 1998, should provide a fresh crop of media reviews.

CHRONOLOGY

World events	Author's life	Literary events
	1934 Born in Yorkshire	**1934** Robert Graves, *I, Claudius;* T.S. Eliot, *The Rock*
		1935 T.S. Eliot, *Murder in the Cathedral*
1936 Accession of Edward VIII; abdication of Edward VIII and accession of George VI; Jarrow to London march; start of Spanish Civil War		
1937 Neville Chamberlain becomes British Prime Minister		**1937** George Orwell, *The Road to Wigan Pier*
1939-45 Second World War		**1939** James Joyce, *Finnegans Wake*
1940 Winston Churchill becomes British Prime Minister		
1945 Clement Atlee becomes British Prime Minister		**1945** Evelyn Waugh, *Brideshead Revisited;* George Orwell, *Animal Farm;* Philip Larkin, *The North Ship;* J.B. Priestley, *An Inspector calls*
1946 National Insurance Act establishes comprehensive insurance system based on Beveridge scheme; National Health Act provides free health care to all; Bank of England and coal industry nationalised; Cold War begins		
1947 Economic crisis in Britain; USA offers Marshall Aid to Europe; partition of India		
		1948 Graham Greene, *The Heart of the Matter*
		1949 Ivy Compton-Burnett, *Two Worlds and their Ways;* George Orwell, *Nineteen Eighty-four*
1951 Winston Churchill becomes British Prime Minister; Festival of Britain		**1951-75** Anthony Powell, *A Dance to the Music of Time*
1952 Death of George VI; accession of Elizabeth II		**1952** Samuel Beckett, *Waiting for Godot*

World events	Author's life	Literary events
		1954 Iris Murdoch, *Under the Net;* William Golding, *Lord of the Flies;* Kingsley Amis, *Lucky Jim;* Dylan Thomas, *Under Milkwood;* · Tennessee Williams, *Cat on a Hot Tin Roof*
1955 Anthony Eden becomes British Prime Minister; West Indian immigration to Britain increases		**1955** Kingsley Amis, *That Uncertain Feeling*
1956 Suez crisis; beginning of rock and roll music		**1956** John Osborne, *Look Back in Anger*
1957 Harold Macmillan becomes British Prime Minister; Wolfenden report on homosexuality and prostitution		**1957** Harold Pinter, *The Birthday Party*
		1958 Alan Sillitoe, *Saturday Night and Sunday Morning;* Samuel Beckett, *Krapp's Last Stand*
		1959 Alan Sillitoe, *The Loneliness of the Long-Distance Runner;* Arnold Wesker, *Roots*
1960 Macmillan makes 'Wind of Change' speech	**1960** *Beyond the Fringe;* Lecturer at Magdalen College, University of Oxford (till 1962)	**1960** Kingsley Amis, *Take a Girl Like You;* John Betjeman, *Summoned by Bells*
1961 Berlin Wall built		**1961** Samuel Beckett, *Happy Days*
1962 Commonwealth Immigrants Act passed to control numbers of immigrants; end of post-war National Service		**1962** Doris Lessing, *The Golden Notebook;* Anthony Burgess, *A Clockwork Orange;* Edith Sitwell, *The Outcasts*
1963 President Kennedy assassinated; Profumo scandal; Macmillan resigns; Alec Douglas-Home becomes British Prime Minister		**1963** John le Carré, *The Spy Who Came in from the Cold*
1964 Harold Wilson becomes British Prime Minister; Commons vote to end Death Penalty		**1964** John Osborne, *Inadmissable Evidence;* Samuel Beckett, *How It Is;* Joe Orton, *Entertaining Mr Sloane*

World events	Author's life	Literary events
1965 Race Relations Act sets up Race Relations Board		
1966 England wins World Cup	**1966** *On the Margin*	**1966** Graham Greene, *The Comedians;* Tom Stoppard, *Rosencrantz and Guildenstern Are Dead*
		1966-75 Paul Scott, *The Raj Quartet*
1967 Homosexual acts between consenting adults legalised in England and Wales		**1967** Ted Hughes, *Wodwo;* Joe Orton, *Loot*
1968 Enoch Powell's controversial speech on immigration		
1969 Legal age for right to vote reduced from 21 to 18; Divorce Reform Act makes breakdown of marriage cause for divorce; *Apollo 11* lands on the moon	**1969** *Forty Years On*	**1969** W.H. Auden, *City Without Walls;* Joe Orton, *What the Butler Saw;* John Fowles, *The French Lieutenant's Woman*
1970 Edward Heath becomes British Prime Minister; many strikes in protest at Industrial Relations Bill; emergency power cuts		
1971 Introduction of decimal currency; 'Angry Brigade' bombs home of Secretary of State for Employment		**1971** John Osborne, *West of Suez*
1972 Miners' strike; 'Bloody Sunday'; Britain joins the Common Market	**1972** *Getting On*	
1973 Three Day Week introduced to save energy	**1973** *Habeas Corpus*	**1973** Martin Amis, *The Rachel Papers*
1974 Harold Wilson becomes British Prime Minister; inflation reaches 16%		**1974** John le Carré, *Tinker, Tailor, Soldier, Spy;* Philip Larkin, *High Windows;* Tom Stoppard, *Travesties*
1975 Inflation reaches 25%; Equal Opportunities Commission established; Margaret Thatcher becomes leader of the Conservative Party		

World events	Author's life	Literary events
1976 Jim Callaghan becomes British Prime Minister		
1977 Aircraft and shipbuilding industries nationalised; Queen Elizabeth's Silver Jubilee	**1977** *The Old Country*	**1977** Martin Amis, *Dark Secrets*
1979 Margaret Thatcher becomes Britain's first woman Prime Minister		**1979** Ted Hughes, *Moortown;* Harold Pinter, *Betrayal;* Caryl Churchill, *Cloud Nine*
1980 Unemployment more than 2 million	**1980** *Enjoy*	**1980** Iris Murdoch, *Nuns and Soldiers*
1981 Social Democratic Party is formed	**1981** *Office Suite*	**1981** John Osborne, *A Better Class of Person;* Samuel Beckett, *Ohio Impromptu;* Salman Rushdie, *Midnight's Children*
1982 Falkland Island Crisis	**1982** *Objects of Affection and Other Plays*	**1982** Malcolm Bradbury, *The After Dinner Game;* Caryl Churchill, *Top Girls;* Alan Bleasdale, *Boys from the Black Stuff*
1983 Sir Roy Griffiths's report, NHS Management Inquiry	**1983** *An Englishman Abroad*	**1983** Fay Weldon, *The Life and Loves of a She-Devil;* Salman Rushdie, *Shame*
1983 on Privatizations of British Telecom, British Gas, British Airways, British Petroleum; sale of council houses; reform of domestic rates into Community Charge (Poll Tax)		
1984 IRA attack Conservative Party conference at Brighton **1984-5** Miners' strike		**1984** William Golding, *The Paper Men;* Tom Stoppard, *The Real Thing;* Julian Barnes, *Flaubert's Parrot*
	1985 *The Writer in Disguise*	**1985** Graham Swift, *Waterland;* Jeanette Winterson, *Oranges are not the Only Fruit;* Troy Kennedy Martin, *Edge of Darkness*
	1986 *The Insurance Man*	**1986** Iris Murdoch, *The Good Apprentice;* Graham Swift, *Learning to Swim and Other Stories;* Dennis Potter, *The Singing Detective*

CHRONOLOGY

World events	Author's life	Literary events
1987 Margaret Thatcher becomes first Prime Minister in twentieth century to serve three consecutive terms;	**1987** *Two Kafka Plays*	**1987** Roddy Doyle, *The Commitments*
	1988 *Talking Heads*	**1988** Salman Rushdie, *The Satanic Verses;* Graham Swift, *Out of This World*
1989 NHS reforms unveiled in 1989 White Paper, *Working for Patients*	**1989** *Single Spies*	**1989** Martin Amis, *London Fields;*
1990 NHS and Community Care Act; Poll Tax riots; Margaret Thatcher resigns; John Major becomes Prime Minister	**1990** *The Wind in the Willows*	**1990** David Hare, *Racing Demon*
1991 Gulf War	**1991** *The Madness of George III*	**1991** Angela Carter, *Wise Children*
1992 'Black Monday' stock market crash; Britain withdraws from ERM		**1992** Jeanette Winterson, *Written on the Body*
		1993 Harold Pinter, *Moonlight;* Roddy Doyle, *Paddy Clarke Ha Ha ha;* David Hare, *The Absence of War;* Tom Stoppard, *Arcadia*
	1994 *Writing Home*	**1994** Jeanette Winterson, *Art and Lies*
	1995 *Tour of Westminster Abbey*	**1995** Martin Amis, *The Information;* Salman Rushdie, *The Moor's Last Sigh*
	1996 *The Clothes They Stood Up In*	**1996** Samuel Beckett, *Nohow On*
1997 New Labour wins general election; Tony Blair becomes Prime Minister		
	1998 *Talking Heads II*	

closure the impression of completeness and finality achieved by the ending of some literary works, or parts of literary works: 'and they all lived happily ever after'

colloquialism (Lat. 'like speech') the use of the kinds of expression and grammar associated with ordinary, everyday speech, rather than formal language

deconstruction most of the ideas of deconstruction originate in the difficult works of the French philosopher, Jacques Derrida. He believes that all notions of the existence of an absolute meaning in language are wrong; yet this assumption has dominated Western thought and it should be the aim of the philosopher and critic, Derrida argues, to 'deconstruct' the philosophy and literature of the past to show this false assumption and reveal the essential paradox at the heart of language. To 'deconstruct' a text is merely to show how texts deconstruct themselves because of the fundamental indeterminateness at the core of language. One reason for the difficulty of Derrida's own writing is that he is aware of his own texts deconstructing themselves.

The word 'deconstruction' is now often used merely to refer to the revelation of partially hidden meanings in a text, especially those that illuminate aspects of its relationship with its social and political context. In its weakest form, it has become a jargon word for 'analyse' or 'interpret'

dialect (Gk. 'way of speaking, language of a district) a variation on the English language associated with a particular area

double entendre (Fr. 'hearing twice') double meaning; used in English almost exclusively to imply a pun with a sexual or bawdy meaning

dramatic irony see irony

epic (Gk. 'speech, song, word') an epic is a long narrative poem in elevated style, about the exploits of superhuman heroes. The adjective is often used more casually to mean 'heroic'

feminist criticism Since the late 1960s feminist theories about literature and language, and feminist interpretations of texts, have multiplied enormously. A tenet of feminist thought is that male ways of perceiving and ordering are 'inscribed' into the prevailing ideology of society. This can be disclosed by studying language itself, and texts, in order to discover the characteristic assumptions which are inherent in them. In patriarchal societies – also called 'androcentric (Gk. 'man-centred') or 'phallocratic' (Gk. 'penis-ruled') – language contains binary oppositions of qualities such as active/passive, adventurous/timid, or reasonable/irrational, in which, it is argued, the feminine is always associated with the less desirable words in the listed pairs. Women are subordinated because they are perceived through this constantly repeated framework of negative perceptions which are inherent in language. Areas of human achievement are defined in terms of male ideas and aspirations, and the presumption that advances in civilisation have always been brought about by men. Women are thus conditioned to enter society accepting their own inferiority, and even co-operating in and approving its perpetuation. Femininity is regarded as a construct of society

flashback a term borrowed from films. A sudden jump backwards in time to an earlier episode or scene in a narrative

genre the term for a kind or type of literature. The three major genre of literature are poetry, drama and the novel

irony (Gk. 'dissembling') a manner of speaking or writing that consists of saying one thing whilst meaning another. **Dramatic irony** occurs when the audience of a play knows more than the characters and can therefore foresee the tragic or comic circumstances which are to come

loose sentences casual, conversational prose which is not grammatically highly ordered and which readily splits into short units of sense

metaphor a figure of speech in which a word or phrase is applied to an object or action that it does not literally denote in order to imply a resemblance

monologue, monodrama (Gk. ' speaking alone', 'alone-play') a passage or play for one speaker. Lyric poems, prayers, the soliloquy, are all varieties of monologue

narrator (Lat. 'the teller') to narrate a story is to recount and establish some connection between a series of events. In understanding and commenting upon a story, our attention is immediately focused on the narrator and his or her **point of view**. A **transparent** narrator is one, like those in *Talking Heads*, who reveals more than he or she realises, and an **unreliable** narrator is one whose account of events we have reason to mistrust

parallel (Gk. 'alongside one another') parallels in literature are different works or parts of works that in some way resemble each other, and are therefore useful for the purposes of comparison and contrast. Their similarity may be a matter of subject matter, or an aspect of style or method

parody (Gk. 'mock poem') an imitation of a specific work of literature or style devised so as to ridicule its characteristic features. Exaggeration, or the application of a serious tone to an absurd subject, are typical methods

post-structuralism see structuralism

satire (Lat. 'mixture, medley', from *satis,* enough) literature which exhibits or examines vice and folly and makes them appear ridiculous or contemptible

soliloquy (Lat. 'to speak alone') a dramatic convention, which allows a character in a play to speak directly to the audience, as if thinking aloud

stream of consciousness a narrative technique of modern writing: the attempt to convey all the contents of a character's mind in relation to the stream of experience as it passes by, often at random

structuralism and post-structuralism structuralism examines aspects of human society, including language, literature and social institutions, as integrated structures or systems in which the parts have no real existence of their own, but derive meaning and significance only from their place within the system. For example, the basic unit of meaning in language, the phoneme (basic sound unit), is seen to derive its meaning not from any inherent qualities in itself, but because of its 'difference' from other sounds. Structuralist critics often explore individual works in literature by analysing them in terms of linguistic concepts, like the phoneme, or as if the structure of a work resembled the syntax of a sentence. Others concentrate on examining the conventions and expectations which a knowledgeable reader understands implicitly when reading the work, with the ultimate aim of building up a kind of grammar or ground-plan of the whole system of literature and its place in society

Structuralism has now been superseded by the even more radical post-structuralist theories, also known as deconstruction

subtext a word used for the situation that lies behind the behaviour of characters in a play, but to which no one refers explicitly and which may never be fully explained. The word can also be used to refer to any implicit assumptions or situation that can be discerned behind the manifest and explicit plot of a narrative or poem

symbol (Gk. 'mark, sign, token', originally 'put together') a symbol is something which represents something else (often an idea or quality) by analogy or association. Writers use conventional symbols (white=innocence; lion=courage; rose=beauty) but also they invent their own

tone tone is a critical concept which implies that written literature is like speech, requiring a speaker and a listener, tone being the attitude adopted by the speaker to the listener

tragicomedy a mixture of tragedy and comedy

transparent narrator see narrator

unreliable narrator see narrator

verbatim (Lat. *Verbum,* 'word') in exactly the same words, word for word

AUTHOR OF THIS NOTE

Delia Dick was one of the first graduates of the Open University and a post-graduate at the University of Warwick. She has taught at various levels and at present lectures in English Literature at Coventry University. She is the author of the Advanced York Notes on Jane Austen's *Mansfield Park.*

NOTES

NOTES

NOTES

NOTES

NOTES

NOTES

NOTES

ADVANCED LEVEL TITLES

York Notes Advanced (£3.99 each)

Margaret Atwood
The Handmaid's Tale

Jane Austen
Mansfield Park

Jane Austen
Persuasion

Jane Austen
Pride and Prejudice

Alan Bennett
Talking Heads

William Blake
Songs of Innocence and of Experience

Charlotte Brontë
Jane Eyre

Emily Brontë
Wuthering Heights

Geoffrey Chaucer
The Franklin's Tale

Geoffrey Chaucer
General Prologue to the Canterbury Tales

Geoffrey Chaucer
The Wife of Bath's Prologue and Tale

Joseph Conrad
Heart of Darkness

Charles Dickens
Great Expectations

John Donne
Selected Poems

George Eliot
The Mill on the Floss

F. Scott Fitzgerald
The Great Gatsby

E.M. Forster
A Passage to India

Brian Friel
Translations

Thomas Hardy
The Mayor of Casterbridge

Thomas Hardy
Tess of the d'Urbervilles

Seamus Heaney
Selected Poems from Opened Ground

Nathaniel Hawthorne
The Scarlet Letter

James Joyce
Dubliners

John Keats
Selected Poems

Christopher Marlowe
Doctor Faustus

Arthur Miller
Death of a Salesman

Toni Morrison
Beloved

William Shakespeare
Antony and Cleopatra

William Shakespeare
As You Like It

William Shakespeare
Hamlet

William Shakespeare
King Lear

William Shakespeare
Measure for Measure

William Shakespeare
The Merchant of Venice

William Shakespeare
Much Ado About Nothing

William Shakespeare
Othello

William Shakespeare
Romeo and Juliet

William Shakespeare
The Tempest

William Shakespeare
The Winter's Tale

Mary Shelley
Frankenstein

Alice Walker
The Color Purple

Oscar Wilde
The Importance of Being Earnest

Tennessee Williams
A Streetcar Named Desire

John Webster
The Duchess of Malfi

W.B. Yeats
Selected Poems

GCSE and equivalent levels (£3.50 each)

Maya Angelou
I Know Why the Caged Bird Sings

Jane Austen
Pride and Prejudice

Alan Ayckbourn
Absent Friends

Elizabeth Barrett Browning
Selected Poems

Robert Bolt
A Man for All Seasons

Harold Brighouse
Hobson's Choice

Charlotte Brontë
Jane Eyre

Emily Brontë
Wuthering Heights

Shelagh Delaney
A Taste of Honey

Charles Dickens
David Copperfield

Charles Dickens
Great Expectations

Charles Dickens
Hard Times

Charles Dickens
Oliver Twist

Roddy Doyle
Paddy Clarke Ha Ha Ha

George Eliot
Silas Marner

George Eliot
The Mill on the Floss

William Golding
Lord of the Flies

Oliver Goldsmith
She Stoops To Conquer

Willis Hall
The Long and the Short and the Tall

Thomas Hardy
Far from the Madding Crowd

Thomas Hardy
The Mayor of Casterbridge

Thomas Hardy
Tess of the d'Urbervilles

Thomas Hardy
The Withered Arm and other Wessex Tales

L.P. Hartley
The Go-Between

Seamus Heaney
Selected Poems

Susan Hill
I'm the King of the Castle

Barry Hines
A Kestrel for a Knave

Louise Lawrence
Children of the Dust

Harper Lee
To Kill a Mockingbird

Laurie Lee
Cider with Rosie

Arthur Miller
The Crucible

Arthur Miller
A View from the Bridge

Robert O'Brien
Z for Zachariah

Frank O'Connor
My Oedipus Complex and other stories

George Orwell
Animal Farm

J.B. Priestley
An Inspector Calls

Willy Russell
Educating Rita

Willy Russell
Our Day Out

J.D. Salinger
The Catcher in the Rye

William Shakespeare
Henry IV Part 1

William Shakespeare
Henry V

William Shakespeare
Julius Caesar

William Shakespeare
Macbeth

William Shakespeare
The Merchant of Venice

William Shakespeare
A Midsummer Night's Dream

William Shakespeare
Much Ado About Nothing

William Shakespeare
Romeo and Juliet

William Shakespeare
The Tempest

William Shakespeare
Twelfth Night

George Bernard Shaw
Pygmalion

Mary Shelley
Frankenstein

R.C. Sherriff
Journey's End

Rukshana Smith
Salt on the snow

John Steinbeck
Of Mice and Men

Robert Louis Stevenson
Dr Jekyll and Mr Hyde

Jonathan Swift
Gulliver's Travels

Robert Swindells
Daz 4 Zoe

Mildred D. Taylor
Roll of Thunder, Hear My Cry

Mark Twain
Huckleberry Finn

James Watson
Talking in Whispers

William Wordsworth
Selected Poems

A Choice of Poets

Mystery Stories of the Nineteenth Century including The Signalman

Nineteenth Century Short Stories

Poetry of the First World War

Six Women Poets

Chinua Achebe
Things Fall Apart

Edward Albee
Who's Afraid of Virginia Woolf?

Margaret Atwood
Cat's Eye

Jane Austen
Emma

Jane Austen
Northanger Abbey

Jane Austen
Sense and Sensibility

Samuel Beckett
Waiting for Godot

Robert Browning
Selected Poems

Robert Burns
Selected Poems

Angela Carter
Nights at the Circus

Geoffrey Chaucer
The Merchant's Tale

Geoffrey Chaucer
The Miller's Tale

Geoffrey Chaucer
The Nun's Priest's Tale

Samuel Taylor Coleridge
Selected Poems

Daniel Defoe
Moll Flanders

Daniel Defoe
Robinson Crusoe

Charles Dickens
Bleak House

Charles Dickens
Hard Times

Emily Dickinson
Selected Poems

Carol Ann Duffy
Selected Poems

George Eliot
Middlemarch

T.S. Eliot
The Waste Land

T.S. Eliot
Selected Poems

Henry Fielding
Joseph Andrews

E.M. Forster
Howards End

John Fowles
The French Lieutenant's Woman

Robert Frost
Selected Poems

Elizabeth Gaskell
North and South

Stella Gibbons
Cold Comfort Farm

Graham Greene
Brighton Rock

Thomas Hardy
Jude the Obscure

Thomas Hardy
Selected Poems

Joseph Heller
Catch-22

Homer
The Iliad

Homer
The Odyssey

Gerard Manley Hopkins
Selected Poems

Aldous Huxley
Brave New World

Kazuo Ishiguro
The Remains of the Day

Ben Jonson
The Alchemist

Ben Jonson
Volpone

James Joyce
A Portrait of the Artist as a Young Man

Philip Larkin
Selected Poems

D.H. Lawrence
The Rainbow

D.H. Lawrence
Selected Stories

D.H. Lawrence
Sons and Lovers

D.H. Lawrence
Women in Love

John Milton
Paradise Lost Bks I & II

John Milton
Paradise Lost Bks IV & IX

Thomas More
Utopia

Sean O'Casey
Juno and the Paycock

George Orwell
Nineteen Eighty-four

John Osborne
Look Back in Anger

Wilfred Owen
Selected Poems

Sylvia Plath
Selected Poems

Alexander Pope
Rape of the Lock and other poems

Ruth Prawer Jhabvala
Heat and Dust

Jean Rhys
Wide Sargasso Sea

William Shakespeare
As You Like It

William Shakespeare
Coriolanus

William Shakespeare
Henry IV Pt 1

William Shakespeare
Henry V

William Shakespeare
Julius Caesar

William Shakespeare
Macbeth

William Shakespeare
Measure for Measure

William Shakespeare
A Midsummer Night's Dream

William Shakespeare
Richard II

William Shakespeare
Richard III

William Shakespeare
Sonnets

William Shakespeare
The Taming of the Shrew

FUTURE TITLES (continued)

William Shakespeare
Twelfth Night

William Shakespeare
The Winter's Tale

George Bernard Shaw
Arms and the Man

George Bernard Shaw
Saint Joan

Muriel Spark
The Prime of Miss Jean Brodie

John Steinbeck
The Grapes of Wrath

John Steinbeck
The Pearl

Tom Stoppard
Arcadia

Tom Stoppard
Rosencrantz and Guildenstern are Dead

Jonathan Swift
Gulliver's Travels and The Modest Proposal

Alfred, Lord Tennyson
Selected Poems

W.M. Thackeray
Vanity Fair

Virgil
The Aeneid

Edith Wharton
The Age of Innocence

Tennessee Williams
Cat on a Hot Tin Roof

Tennessee Williams
The Glass Menagerie

Virginia Woolf
Mrs Dalloway

Virginia Woolf
To the Lighthouse

William Wordsworth
Selected Poems

Metaphysical Poets

York Notes – the Ultimate Literature Guides

York Notes are recognised as the best literature study guides.
If you have enjoyed using this book and have found it useful, you
can now order others directly from us – simply follow the ordering
instructions below.

HOW TO ORDER

Decide which title(s) you require and then order in one of the following
ways:

Booksellers
All titles available from good bookstores.

By post
List the title(s) you require in the space provided overleaf,
select your method of payment, complete your name and
address details and return your completed order form and
payment to:

> *Addison Wesley Longman Ltd*
> *PO BOX 88*
> *Harlow*
> *Essex CM19 5SR*

By phone
Call our Customer Information Centre on 01279 623923 to
place your order, quoting mail number: HEYN1.

By fax
Complete the order form overleaf, ensuring you fill in your
name and address details and method of payment, and fax it
to us on 01279 414130.

By e-mail
E-mail your order to us on awlhe.orders@awl.co.uk listing
title(s) and quantity required and providing full name and
address details as requested overleaf. Please quote mail
number: HEYN1. Please do not send credit card details by
e-mail.

York Notes Order Form

Titles required:

Quantity	Title/ISBN	Price

Sub total _____

Please add £2.50 postage & packing _____

(P & P is free for orders over £50) _____

Total _____

Mail no: HEYN1

Your Name _____

Your Address _____

Postcode _____   Telephone _____

Method of payment

☐ I enclose a cheque or a P/O for £_____ made payable to Addison Wesley Longman Ltd

☐ Please charge my Visa/Access/AMEX/Diners Club card
Number _____   Expiry Date _____
Signature _____   Date _____

(please ensure that the address given above is the same as for your credit card)

Prices and other details are correct at time of going to press but may change without notice. All orders are subject to status.

☐ *Please tick this box if you would like a complete listing of Longman Study Guides (suitable for GCSE and A-level students)*

York Press

Longman

Addison Wesley Longman